More Praise for *Montana Campfire Tales*

"No one in Montana today knows the history of the state as well as Dave Walter does. These campfire stories truly make our history come alive, putting flesh on the bones of the usual narratives."

—Michael Malone, author of
*The Battle for Butte: Mining and Politics on
the Northern Frontier, 1864-1906*

"In these fourteen essays, Dave Walter gives us what K. Ross Toole repeatedly called for: grass-roots history that both entertains and educates. More than a skilled historian, Walter is the consummate storyteller. Whether setting background to the ongoing "wolf wars," recounting tragic episodes in relations between the races in Montana, or describing the real-life adventures of some of the territory's and the state's most colorful characters, Walter tells his stories in graphic detail—often tinging the tale with his wry humor. Walter has chosen his stories craftily; each one is steeped in human interest, and in the hands of this masterful historian/storyteller, that interest is raised to its most engaging level."

—Linda Peavey and Ursula Smith, authors of
*Women in Waiting in the Western
Movement: Life on the Home Frontier*

"Made from Montana's unique historical mosaic, this exceptionally well-tailored collection has deep pockets lined with the finest storytelling fabric in the state."

—Darrell Robes Kipp
Piegan Institute

OTHER BOOKS BY DAVE WALTER

Christmastime In Montana

Today Then: America's Best Minds Look 100 Years into the Future on the Occasion of the 1893 World's Columbian Exposition

Will Man Fly? Strange and Wonderful Predictions from the 1890s

CO-AUTHOR:

More from the Quarries of Last Chance Gulch, Volume 1

More from the Quarries of Last Chance Gulch, Volume 2

MONTANA CAMPFIRE TALES

fourteen historical narratives

Dave Walter

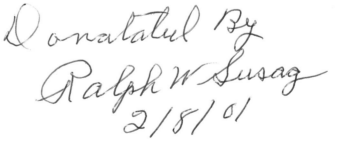

TWODOT

Helena, Montana

A · TWODOT · BOOK

© 1997 by Dave Walter
Published by Falcon® Publishing, Inc.
Helena, Montana

10 9 8 7 6 5 4

Printed in the United States of America.

Library of Congress Cataloging-in-Publication Data:
Walter, David, 1943-
    Montana campfire tales : fourteen historical narratives / by Dave Walter
        p.   cm.
    ISBN 1-56044-539-4 (pbk.)
    1. Montana—History—Anecdotes. 2. Montana—Biography—Anecdotes.
I. Title
F731.6.W35 1997
978.6—dc21   97-19135
                                                                              CIP

You can order extra copies of this book and get information and prices for other
TwoDot books by writing to Falcon,® P.O. Box 1718, Helena, MT 59624, or
calling 1-800-582-2665. Also, please ask for a free copy of our current catalog
listing all Falcon® books. To contact us via e-mail, visit our home page at http://
www.falconguide.com.

Cover photo credits:
Lower left: Truman C. Everts. Montana Historical Society, Helena. Upper left:
Rescue workers, Going-to-the-Sun Road avalanche, 1953. Glacier National Park
Museum, West Glacier, Montana. Upper right: Carrie Nation. Kansas State
Historical Society. Center right, front cover, and center left, back cover: Killing of
bison, ca. 1879. L. A. Huffman, photographer. Montana Historical Society, Hel-
ena. Bottom: Piegan camp on river bottom, no date. Dan Dutro, photographer.
Montana Historical Society, Helena.

This work is dedicated to my parents,
George and Dorothy Walter,
who taught me the importance
of people and place
and warned me about the intricate
interactions of the two.

CONTENTS

INTRODUCTION

The genuine vigor of Western history survives today in the arena of local history. Here stalwart, robust, truly exciting people lived, and fundamental, pivotal, amazing events occurred. Through local history, Montanans glimpse the real characters and incidents of the past—ones that lived and occurred on familiar ground. When Montanans attempt to define "a sense of place," local history provides depth to the context.

The outspoken Western historian K. Ross Toole occasionally referred to the *telling* of Montana history—"the Montana story"—as a fractured mirror: a composite of contiguous, disproportionate, yet neatly arranged shards. By extension, the large shards represent major events/people/movements, and the smaller fragments exemplify the less well-known episodes in Montana history. Toole always emphasized, however, that even when one captures the sparkling glass pieces within a frame, the mosaic presents a somewhat distorted image.

In his historical writing, Toole liked to hurl about the larger shards: the Lewis and Clark expedition; the "Hard Winter of 1886-1887"; the War of the Copper Kings; the homesteader boom; strippable prairie coal. Yet, as a mentor of scores of graduate students, he challenged them to investigate, scrub, and polish the smaller, irregularly shaped, less-well-known fragments.

Toole's challenge is really the challenge of local history: to research thoroughly a topic of local focus and impact; to present it intelligibly; to place it in a larger historical context. This is grassroots history. Moreover, it must be completed *before* the synthesizing historian conscientiously can generate broad generalizations and sweeping characterizations.

With the polishing of each little, uncovered account, the fractured mirror projects "the Montana story" a bit more clearly, a bit more brightly, a bit more honestly. In an era of dreadful Western stereotypes, local historical people and local historical events constitute Montanans' primary anchors to the truth.

Local history feeds the "Montana story." It tells Montanans something about who they are, by explaining to them something about where they have been. This is not precise science; it is not chemistry, biology, or even geology. Local history is researched storytelling. It rests much closer to the oral tradition than many academic historians would like to admit.

As such, local history is *always* susceptible to review and revision. The larger shards of story particularly sustain repeated tellings, because the perspective of the person looking in the mirror keeps changing. Many of the smaller shards simply need truthful telling.

This volume combines fourteen Montana accounts—a few recollective, but most untold—which span a century of Montana history. Each of these episodes has appeared in Montana Magazine, but they never have been compiled under a single cover. Every one of the selections is a Montana story that just as readily could be told in front of a crackling, sparking campfire—complete with shifting clouds of wood smoke and dancing shafts of firelight.

Although these tales are small, uneven pieces of the fractured mirror, they are basic to "the Montana story" since they reveal several themes deeply woven into the Montana fabric. For example:

▲ The most severe ethical burden that the white Montanan

currently shoulders is the federal government's historical treatment of the Native American during the last 150 years. The thread of native-white conflict winds through the stories of the Thomas tragedy, the Baker Massacre, the life of Louis Riel, and the shooting of Warden Charles Peyton.

▲ The relationship of human beings to their environment undergirds "the Montana story"—as they suffer from it, battle it, struggle to understand it, adapt to it, and receive spiritual energy from it. This relationship creates a consistent line that twists through the adventures of Sir St. George Gore, Truman Everts's agony in Yellowstone, the history of the wolf in Montana, and a deadly avalanche on Going-to-the-Sun Road.

▲ Montana history is rife with interpersonal conflicts— Montanans fighting each other over political programs and solutions, cultural values, economic priorities, interracial differences, moral and ethical standards. The thread of these conflicts warps through the flight of Coxey's Army, Butte's reception of Carry Nation, the impeachment of Judge Crum, and the plight of Japanese workers in Montana during World War II.

In addition to these thematic threads, many of the fourteen stories reflect the lighter, ironic, everyday component of the Montana past. Montana history remains a perpetual wellspring of overt humor and frivolity. Is Sir St. George Gore, camped in Continental luxury on the Tongue River, more ridiculous than Carry Nation busting into Butte's ABC Dance Hall? Who or what, indeed, *is* the "Petrified Man"? How *should* President Cleveland have responded, once the Coxeyites stole the train and headed down the Yellowstone? How did Montana produce a bank-robbing gang to rival Bonnie and Clyde? Above all, these are stories of Montana people—and Montana people never fail to be wondrously fallible and entertaining!

Ross Toole also noted that local history, when practiced effectively, provides both entertainment and education, plus a reminder of man's basic humanity through time. These fourteen small, irregular shards add clarity and a bit of light to the fractured-mirror telling of "the Montana story." And, most certainly, "the Montana story" is the business of us all. Jean Sullivan, as he lies buried in the hard-packed avalanche snow on Going-to-the-Sun Road waiting for rescue, correctly asserts: "We are in this together. . . . We are in this together. . . ."

For the creation of these fourteen pieces, and for dozens of others, I am deeply indebted to the long-time editor of *Montana Magazine*, Carolyn Cunningham. In what was nothing if not a mindless leap of faith, Carolyn accepted a manuscript article from me in 1983 *and paid me for it!*

Over a decade, on fifty subsequent manuscripts, Carolyn performed the magic of a gifted editor—suggesting, interpreting, cajoling, clarifying, understanding, persisting, insisting. She finally shaped me into a writer of whom she could be proud—or at least one who would not embarrass her publicly! Carolyn Cunningham opened doors for me, as well as my eyes to commercial writing. She remains one hell of an editor and a great friend. I will be grateful to her always.

Two members of the same editing profession are primarily responsible for the development and production of this volume. Rick Newby and Noelle Sullivan at Falcon Press represent the best of the profession, particularly in assessing and querying. The cohesion evident in this work of storytelling is the result of their perception, knowledge, experience, and sensitivity. Again, I have been most fortunate.

This work has suffered several false starts. That it finally has reached publication is solely due to the experienced counsel of Marilyn Grant, yet another superb editor and an agent-in-training. I could not have been placed in kinder or more knowledgeable hands.

I am further indebted for these fourteen pieces to an institution. The Montana Historical Society, in what remains an inexplicable move, hired me in 1979 to sit the reference desk in its library. For almost fifteen years, the position introduced me to thousands of bits of Montana history that no rational person would have sought on his own. It also acquainted me with scores of devoted, curious Montana local historians who have sparked so much of my interest in, and my love for, Montana history.

In addition, that job introduced me to the truly remarkable published and archival resources held by the Society. Some of the most instructive, rewarding, and enjoyable hours of my life have been spent immersed in those materials. For providing me with a wondrous position—in which I invariably learned two or three extraordinary things each day—I am deeply obliged to the Society. For allowing me to remain at the Society, as its research historian, I am even more grateful.

Finally, I owe the largest debt to my family. Every part-time writer pilfers time from friends and loved ones, while endlessly struggling with remorse. I am blessed with an indulgent family—particularly daughters Emily and Amanda—who proffer unconditional (although not always uncritical) understanding. They continue to help me see the world through young eyes, an increasingly difficult task.

My parents, George and Dorothy Walter, submerged me in the West, then challenged me to explore its literature and history. Despite some long, certainly disappointing and dreary years, their faith in me never wavered. How fortunate I have been.

To my wife Marcella I owe the most. She has worked with these fourteen pieces from inception to compilation—never failing to contribute insight and expertise to their development. To an invariably testy writer, she somehow imparts perspective, advice, and confidence without compromising her integrity. Again, thank you, dear.

CHAPTER 1

SIR ST. GEORGE GORE: ELEGANT VICTORIAN AND SLOB HUNTER

From 1854 to 1857, Sir St. George Gore hunted lands in what are now the states of Colorado, Wyoming, Montana, and the Dakotas. This foreign nimrod shot game in a style and to an extreme that have never been duplicated here. The derivation of the noun "gore"—a caked mass of filth or dirt, particularly thick or clotted blood—cannot be traced specifically to the family of Sir St. George. Nevertheless, this English baronet's sporting extravaganza in the American West certainly makes the association plausible.

The Gore line long had been entrenched in the English aristocracy. The baronetcy had existed since the early seventeenth century and controlled vast estates in northwestern Ireland, consolidated around the Manor Gore, near Sligo. George was born to this line in 1811. His family educated him at Winchester School and at Oriel College, Oxford. In the tradition of an aristocrat, he then took the "Grand Tour" of the Continent.

When George reached thirty-one years (in 1842), his father died, and the family title devolved upon him, the eighth baronet of Manor Gore. He established residence in the family's Victorian mansion on fashionable Brunswick Square in the seaside resort of Brighton, East Sussex, about fifty miles south of London.

The new baronet was a stocky, hearty bachelor, fully bearded but prematurely balding. He meshed a thorough knowledge of classical literature, music, and art with a love of the outdoors. Gore became a member of England's elite Turf Club and the Royal Yacht Squadron; while still a young man, he gained a reputation as a skilled horseman, hunter, and fisherman.

Sir St. George Gore proved a sportsman, a scholar, and a gentleman—as well as an excellent judge of Irish whiskey. He also exhibited a fiery temper on occasion. Income from the family's Irish land holdings annually exceeded $200,000, although Gore seldom visited the family manor and relied on a resident manager to handle his Irish operations. To the hilt, Sir St. George personified the Victorian aristocrat.

In English sporting circles, Gore met Sir William Drummond Stewart, the seventh baronet of Murthly, Scotland. Sir William had toured the American West extensively from 1833 to 1838 and then again in 1843. The combination of Stewart's trophies and his stories of wilderness adventure fired Gore's imagination. So, in 1853, Sir St. George determined to organize his own expedition to the Great Plains and the Rocky Mountains.

Gore arranged his American tour through the London office of the American Fur Company, headquartered in St. Louis, Missouri. In the mid-nineteenth century, this company dominated all commerce in the upper Missouri River Valley. Its leader, Pierre Chouteau, Jr., encouraged and supported any project that might ultimately develop wilderness resources and, not incidentally, benefit the company.

When Gore explained that he intended to spend two years hunting, fishing, and exploring in the American interior, the American Fur Company agreed to perform several services for him. It would provide the latest maps of the region and use its St. Louis office to hire experienced frontiersmen for Gore's party. It would also supply Gore's expedition from its posts scattered throughout the West, and exchange U.S. currency at any of its posts for drafts on Gore's London bank. Thus Sir St. George laid the foundation for a fabulous tour in the New World.

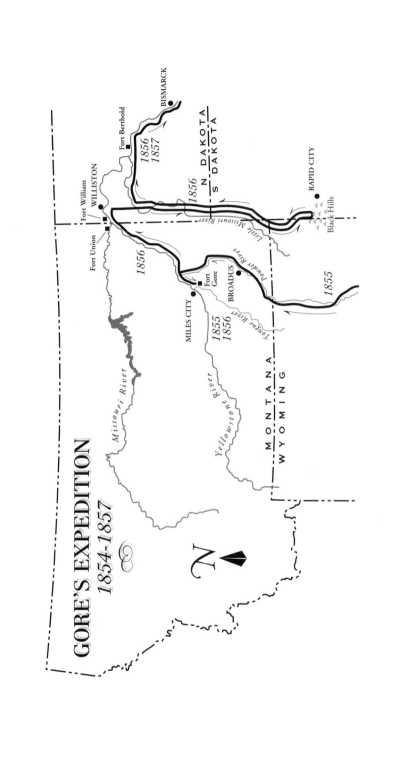

GORE'S EXPEDITION
1854-1857

N

BISMARCK

Fort Berthold

1856
1857

N DAKOTA
S DAKOTA

1856

Fort William
WILLISTON

Fort Union

1856

Little Missouri River

RAPID CITY

Black Hills

Fort Gore

BROADUS

Powder River

1855

MILES CITY

1855
1856

Tongue River

Missouri River

Yellowstone River

MONTANA
WYOMING

Late in January 1854, the forty-two-year-old baronet, his valet, his dog handler and pack of fifty hunting hounds, and his immense cache of crated supplies and equipment sailed from Southhampton, bound for New York City and ultimately St. Louis. The party disembarked in New York harbor in February and reached St. Louis on March 12, 1854. Sir St. George registered at the Planter's House, that frontier city's most elaborate hotel, and prepared for his overland journey.

Gore introduced himself at the headquarters of the American Fur Company, where executives received him warmly. He cashed bank drafts on his Baring Brothers/London account for more than $8,500 in U.S. currency, which he used to purchase additional supplies for the trip. Through the company's office, Gore interviewed and hired forty men with wilderness experience to make the first leg of the journey to Fort Laramie.

The baronet offered the standard rates for specialized work: camp tenders and teamsters at $200-$300; cooks, carpenters, and blacksmiths at $300-$500; guides and hunters at $600. Gore planned to dismiss the men at Fort Laramie in the fall and pay them in American currency. He would reward an employee's exemplary service with a generous bonus and would rehire him in the spring of 1855, for the next leg of the expedition into the Yellowstone Valley.

Gore's coup was the hiring of the already legendary, fifty-year-old mountain man/explorer Jim Bridger through the auspices of the Company. Bridger had traveled the Rocky Mountain region for more than thirty years. He had discovered the Great Salt Lake in 1823 and led several large fur expeditions into the Rockies. In 1843 he established Fort Bridger on the Oregon Trail, and he had just lost that post to Mormon zealots. Bridger had returned to St. Louis, looking for a job. Gore offered him the top wage of five dollars per day to serve as his personal guide for the entire expedition. The two men would become fast friends, despite their many obvious differences in education, experience, and perspective.

Just before leaving St. Louis, Sir St. George visited the office of

Alfred Cumming, the U.S. government's superintendent of Indian Affairs for the Central Division. Because Gore was not an American citizen, federal law required that he obtain a permit to enter Indian country.

Gore's passport allowed him to travel west to Fort Laramie, then north into the Yellowstone Valley, and finally from Fort Union—an American Fur Company post near the mouth of the Yellowstone River—down the Missouri River to St. Louis. The permit expired in the fall of 1856, by which time the baronet planned to complete his circuitous tour.

By mid-June 1854, Gore's party had assembled in Westport (present-day Kansas City), Missouri. His stock had been branded and his vehicles freshly painted and loaded. In the company of Jim Bridger and forty experienced frontiersmen, the aristocrat could barely control his anticipation. The great hunting excursion to the American West was about to begin.

The caravan that pulled out of Westport, heading up the Oregon Trail, resembled nothing that the area had ever seen before or has seen since. It included more than 110 horses, 20 yoke of oxen, 50 hunting hounds, and 28 vehicles. The line began with three mounted guides, who were responsible for picking camping and grazing sites and for shooting game for camp meat. Next came Sir St. George Gore's personal two-horse carriage, painted bright yellow and transported more than six thousand miles from England. This canvas-covered oddity rode high off the ground, with Gore comfortably ensconced on its wide leather seat. Jim Bridger perched on the elevated driver's seat, from where he handled the team and served as a general tour guide. If necessary, by turning cranks at the carriage's four corners, the vehicle could be converted into enclosed sleeping quarters, with the seats folding into a bed. Because of the carriage's smooth ride, Gore carried his barometers, compasses, chronometers, and sextants in the boot.

Following the carriage wound a line of twenty-one modified Red

River carts. These two-wheeled, single-horse carts had been painted shocking red and sported canvas covers. Sixteen of the carts carried the personal baggage of Sir St. George and his servants. The other five carts packed the personal gear of the forty hired men, as well as crates of Indian trade goods, brought from England. These goods included iron kettles, knives, axes, blankets, candles, mirrors, bolts of scarlet and navy calico cloth, bracelets, rings, beads, tin cups and pans, and crude "fusee" firearms. Gore had not received a license to trade in Indian country, so he considered the items gifts—and thought they might extricate him from any tight situations.

Behind the Red River carts rolled four slower-moving Conestoga wagons, each drawn by three pairs of draft horses. The first two vehicles served as mess wagons, carrying tons of preserved food and cooking equipment. The third one contained the blacksmith's and the wheelwright's equipment, and the last Conestoga hauled carpentry tools and assorted hardware.

The final two vehicles in the caravan were high-sided freight wagons, hitched in tandem and pulled by eight yokes of oxen. Each of these wagons hauled ten tons of bulk goods, in crates, barrels, and trunks. Two bullwhackers walked beside the oxen to drive them through the clouds of trail dust.

Following the twenty-eight vehicles plodded the expedition's seventy-five-head stock herd, which included extra horses, oxen, and several cows, so that Gore could enjoy fresh milk with his meals. Herdsmen brought up the rear, but the pack of blooded hunting hounds enjoyed the run of the train, darting under the wagons and racing through the stock herd when not chasing small animals in the high prairie grasses. Eighteen of the dogs were purebred English foxhounds, trained for tracking; the remaining thirty-two animals were greyhounds, bred for the chase. Westerners marveled at the quality of Sir St. George's hunting pack—almost as much as they were envious of his arsenal.

In a region where the quality of a man's firearms could spell the difference between life and death, the baronet's collection of seventy-five custom-made pistols, rifles, and shotguns represented luxury. In Western folk, it produced absolute disbelief. Gore designated one entire Red River cart to haul the variously gauged, heavily decorated, percussion-cap muzzleloaders, handmade by the most skilled English gunsmiths.

Gore also brought an incredible amount of ammunition, remarkable even for a rabid sportsman. He spread the kegs of gunpowder, cases of copper percussion caps, and lead-ball molds through the carts, to prevent an accident from wiping out his supply. The Englishman's mountain man employees simply shook their heads at this quantity of firepower. They had never seen the like for a single pleasure hunt.

Sir St. George's fishing equipment proved equally extensive—and his valet doubled as his fly-tier. One Red River cart carried nothing but fishing gear, which included materials for whatever insect the tier wished to mimic. Since Gore was an excellent fly-fisherman, the camp never wanted for trout. Sport fishing had arrived in the West in exemplary style.

If the quality and abundance of the caravan and its contents amazed Gore's employees, it stupefied other travelers on the Oregon Trail. Wagon trains of determined Mormons bound for the Great Salt Lake, adventurous families headed for the lush valleys of Oregon, and small bands of miners drawn to uncharted placer-gold regions viewed the passing party in disbelief, as if witnessing a medieval procession.

When the Gore contingent made camp for the evening, the display became only more resplendent. After the camp-tenders leveled a choice site, they carefully spread a large India-rubber pad and covered it with a fine French carpet. Over this base the men erected a sixteen-by-twenty-foot, green-and-white-striped, canvas wall tent. This edifice they furnished with several heating stoves, an oval steel bathtub (with the Gore family crest emblazoned on each side), an ornamental brass bedstead, an oak dining table, dinnerware of the finest English pewter, heavy trunks containing the baronet's extensive wardrobe, a large collection of leather-bound classics, and a fur-seated commode with removable pot.

Following several rounds of French wine, Sir St. George Gore enjoyed a multicourse banquet of fresh game and preserved foods, prepared by his cook and served in Continental style by three waiters. Then followed brandy sipping, reading, and conversation with Jim Bridger, a renowned storyteller, before bedtime. The aristocrat seldom retired before midnight or rose before ten in the morning for his bath. During the course of the day's travel, the carriage contingent would overtake the rest of the caravan, which had struck camp as the day began at five o'clock.

Often Gore left the carriage in transit and mounted his statuesque, gray thoroughbred, named Steel Trap, to lope across the plains adjacent to the trail and shoot grouse, antelope, deer, and an occasional bison. After all, this was a hunting trip! Infrequently did the nimrod order his men to carry the quarry back to camp; Gore had come west for the chase and the kill, not for the meat.

The magnificent procession reached Fort Laramie in July 1854 and immediately established a semipermanent camp beside the nearby American Fur Company post, Gratiot's House. After caching the major portion of its supplies and the heavy wagons, the expedition moved southwest into Colorado's Medicine Bow Mountains for a twelve-week hunting and fishing trip.

In the high mountain parks, Gore reveled in the daily bison chase and accumulated several dozen remarkable bison-bull trophies. Led by mountain man Bridger, the party also took bull elk heads, grizzly and black bear hides, wolf pelts, and creels of mountain trout. Upon reaching the Yampa Valley, a friendly band of Ute Indians turned the caravan around, so it worked its way slowly back to Fort Laramie.

At the fort, Gore paid off all but a few of his retinue and settled into winter camp. Bridger then led most of Gore's men back to Missouri down the Oregon Trail. Meanwhile the baronet and his winter crew hunted near Fort Laramie, as weather permitted.

In early May 1855, the Gore party reunited at Fort Laramie for the next leg of the sporting adventure, a trek into Montana's Yellowstone Valley. Again the procession of carriage, carts, wagons, livestock, and hounds took to the prairie, numbering more than forty Americans and guided by Bridger. The caravan moved north through present-day Wyoming until it hit the headwaters of the Powder River. Gore would spend the next twelve months in this northeastern Wyoming/southeastern Montana wilderness—the land of numerous horse-rich Crow bands.

As the party descended the Powder River Valley, the baronet daily fished and hunted its abundant wildlife. He became proficient at the bison chase, darting into stampeding herds atop Steel Trap and dropping the most magnificent lead bulls. For diversion he and the hounds stalked elk, deer, antelope, bighorn sheep, and bear—often killing scores of animals each day. While doing so, Gore never relinquished his standards of European life. He maintained his medieval tent, his daily bath, his catered meals, and his evenings of brandy sipping, journal writing, and reading from the classics.

Jim Bridger was the only employee ever invited to the green-and-white tent to share a Victorian meal or a cordial with the aristocrat. On occasion, Gore would read aloud portions of works by William Shakespeare, Charles Dickens, and Robert Burns to elicit Bridger's comments. Perhaps not surprisingly, the legendary frontiersman chose as his favorite Falstaff in *King Henry IV*. In return, Bridger would regale the baronet with tales of his derring-do in the American West.

In late June, the cavalcade reached the mouth of the Powder River and moved up the Yellowstone Valley to the confluence of the Tongue and Yellowstone Rivers. At the current site of Miles City, the party turned up the Tongue and located a site about twelve miles upstream, where Pumpkin Creek enters. During the summer, Gore's men constructed a substantial fort of upright cottonwood logs. They finished off the interior of "Fort Gore" with log barracks for the men, stables for some of the stock, and cozy private quarters for the baronet.

Meanwhile, Gore, Bridger, the pack of dogs, and a small band of mountain men enjoyed hunting excursions into the game-rich Yellowstone Valley. Slowly Gore realized the isolation and the vulnerability of his relatively small contingent in these vast prairies and valleys. Fortunately the aristocrat's declared association with the American Fur Company and the presence of Bridger led to friendly relations with the local Crow bands.

The group of four dozen men spent the winter of 1855-1856 in comparative quiet at Fort Gore. The baronet hunted bison regularly, often in severe weather, and spent the rest of his time in his toasty warm quarters. Since the Englishman Gore had found it awkward to celebrate the Fourth of July holiday with his men, he celebrated Christmas in elaborate style. His efforts included a large pine tree decorated with Indian trade goods. The men received permission to tap a cask of Irish whiskey, and the baronet lavished gifts on his retinue. Gore even joined the men for Christmas dinner. This remarkable feast consisted of roasted prairie chickens, broiled elk steaks, candied sweet potatoes, creamed corn, hot cinnamon buns, plum pudding, mincemeat pies, and fine French wines.

During the winter, one of Gore's men—a Spaniard known as Uno—died of natural causes. When the men wished to bury their companion in the fur-trade tradition (i.e., wrapped in blankets and laid in a shallow grave), their leader refused. He insisted that Uno receive a proper Christian burial and ordered one of the Red River carts dismantled to provide lumber for the coffin. He further detailed a squad to dig a grave six feet deep—no small chore in the frozen prairie sod. To the party assembled around the grave, Sir St. George Gore read the Twenty-third Psalm from his King James Bible. He then returned to his quarters in respect, and the men filled the grave. Gore would not relinquish his heritage, not even in the face of wilderness expediency.

Another time that same winter, a Piegan raiding party stampeded a portion of the expedition's horse herd, grazing near the fort. Although Gore led a reprisal squad down the Tongue River, he never did recover the stolen horses, about twenty-five percent of his herd. Thereafter he doubled the guard on the herd. About two weeks later, a watchman saw an Indian slipping among the horses. Although he shot and apparently wounded the man, the figure disappeared. The baronet's herd subsequently escaped any raids. In May 1856, Gore led a pack train to a large Crow camp at the head of the Rosebud River to exchange trade goods for two dozen horses, and thus replenished his herd.

In April and May 1856, Gore's hunting excursions increased through the Yellowstone Valley. He seemed possessed by the excitement of the chase, and he shot animals of all kinds, seldom touching the carcass unless it boasted a trophy head. Crow estimates of Gore's harvest during his stay at Fort Gore (July 1855-May 1856) included 105 bears, more than 2,000 bison, and 1,600 elk and deer.

Crow leaders protested this devastation of their food supply to U.S. Indian Agent Alfred Vaughan at Fort Union. Vaughan relayed the information to his St. Louis-based superior, Superintendent of Indian Affairs for the Central Division Alfred Cumming—the same man who, in 1854, had authorized Gore's trip. News of the English sportsman's behavior soon reached Pierre Chouteau, Jr., in his American Fur Company office, and it angered the fur magnate. The company abhorred any disruption of its trading program in the upper Missouri country, and the English aristocrat's actions were decidedly disruptive.

Gore and his men, however, knew nothing of these developments. In May 1856 the baronet ordered his carpenters to construct two flatboats, each ten by twenty-four feet. These craft would carry his bison robes, animal pelts, antlers, and trophy heads downriver to Fort Union—a major American Fur Company post—near the confluence of the Yellowstone and the Missouri Rivers. The rest of the party would trail down the Yellowstone Valley in their caravan, hunting all the way.

Gore intended, upon reaching Fort Union, to dismiss about one-half of his retinue, sell his goods and equipment to the American Fur Company factor, and float the Missouri River to St. Louis with his remaining men and accumulated trophies. He intended to return to England in time for autumn stag hunting in the Scottish Highlands.

The baronet's men torched Fort Gore and left the Tongue River site in mid-May 1856. Because of repeated side trips to hunt, the party did not reach the mouth of the Yellowstone until the end of June. Sir St. George found game plentiful in the lower Yellowstone Valley, and the carts that pulled into camp near Fort Union had animal heads and hides tied all over them. The English baronet had challenged the plains wilderness and survived. His huge collection of trophies proved that he had emerged victorious. Just as important, he had maintained Victorian style and decorum throughout his two-year adventure.

He did not fare as well at Fort Union as he had on the prairies, however. This post served as the American Fur Company's kingpin for its upper Missouri fur trade, and seventy-year-old James Kipp recently had been appointed its factor. Kipp had lived in the West for fifty years and had become an experienced trader and a devoted company man. He had been informed by the St. Louis office that Pierre Chouteau, Jr., and Gore had agreed that the company would provide American currency at Fort Union for the baronet to pay off some of his men. It also would purchase Gore's surplus goods and equipment at "a fair price," and would build two large mackinaw boats to carry the remaining members of the expedition and Gore's trophies to St. Louis.

Yet for months Kipp had heard stories of the devastation that Gore's party had wrought among Yellowstone wildlife populations. The excessive hunting had upset Crow leaders, and the company relied on the Crows as a source of furs and bison hides. Further, in the spring, Kipp had received a visit from the young Piegan Big Plume. He told of being shot by the baronet's men, while "attempting to visit

Fort Gore." Big Plume's complaint carried special weight because he was a brother-in-law of Alexander Culbertson, the company's "King of the Upper Missouri" and Kipp's immediate superior.

So, not surprisingly, the factor received Sir St. George coolly. Nevertheless, Kipp knew his duty. He converted Gore's London drafts into American currency and directed the fort's carpenters to build two mackinaws for the baronet's trip to St. Louis. However, he told the hunter, it would take six weeks to construct these sixty-foot boats, each capable of carrying twenty tons. So the aristocrat paid off more than half of his employees and, with the remaining men, returned to his nearby camp. He would hunt the surrounding prairies and valleys, adding to his already immense trophy collection while he waited.

In the middle of August 1856, Kipp's carpenters completed the two Mackinaws and moored them at the fort. Sir St. George had separated from his stores the provisions he would need for the float to St. Louis. He assembled the bulk of his goods, equipment, vehicles, and livestock in front of the gates to the fort for the negotiations with Kipp. On the appointed afternoon, the factor appeared, and the two men spoke for several minutes. Henry Bostwick, a teamster in Gore's retinue, recalled the incident.

> There was a misunderstanding as to the terms of the bargain, and [Gore] fancied that, in his remoteness from man, the Company was seeking to speculate upon his necessities. He seems to have been mercurial, wrathful, effervescent, and reckless, and heedless of the consequences, he would not stand the terms [that Kipp] prescribed.

Regardless of the cause—if Kipp were practicing some frontier opportunism in the name of the company, or if he wished to punish the aristocrat for his wanton slaughter of wildlife in the name of "sport," or if Gore overestimated the value of his property—the result proved dramatic. An enraged Gore ordered the livestock driven several hundred yards from the fort. He then commanded his men to draw the Conestoga wagons, the Red River carts, and the freight wagons around the elegant carriage—right in front of the gates of the fort. He then personally doused the carriage with lamp oil and touched it off.

As the vehicles caught fire and the flames rose, so did Sir St. George Gore's ire. As if possessed, he began hurling his surplus supplies into the inferno and directed his men to assist. He sacrificed everything to his anger: the green-and-white-striped tent; the brass bedstead; the trunks of clothing and leather-bound books; the French carpets; the magnificent oak table and chairs; the pewterware; the fur-lined commode; the compasses; the chronometers; the sextants; the maps; the kegs of gunpowder; the fishing gear; the excess firearms; what was left of the casks of fine liquor and kegs of trade whiskey; and even the oval bathtub emblazoned with the Gore family crest.

As a crowning act of spite, Gore heaved his elegant leather satchel into the flames. It contained his bank drafts, his passport, his letters of introduction, and his personal journal of the entire expedition. The fire raged all night and into the next day, consuming every last thing and scorching the gates of venerable Fort Union.

As the fire died, the English aristocrat regained control of his temper, if not his good sense. Deep in the wilderness, hundreds of river miles from civilization, he had destroyed precious goods and equipment that could have saved men's lives. Yet even that realization did not assuage Gore's hatred of Kipp and the American Fur Company: he ordered his men to rake the fire's ashes for every scrap of metal and to throw those remains far into the Missouri River, where no one could recover them.

Gore and his men retired to their camp where, after several days, he assessed their situation. He had burned his bank drafts before he could pay for the mackinaws in which he had planned to travel to St. Louis, and he could not purchase the boats because of his spiteful act. So he decided instead to send his two flatboats carrying the trophies down the Missouri, while his party rode the riverside trail almost eighteen hundred miles to St. Louis.

Nevertheless, the more that the Englishman studied a map of the region—provided by Charles Primeau, the factor of Fort William, a non-American Fur Company or "Opposition" post, located near Fort Union—the more he became intrigued with an alternative plan. The flatboats would still go down the Missouri, but Gore, Bridger, and the sixteen men remaining in the retinue—along with their sixty-five horses and fifty hunting dogs—would explore an area marked on the map as "uncharted": the Black Hills. The two contingents would re-unite at the mouth of the Cheyenne River, just above Fort Pierre, and proceed to St. Louis together. Gore believed that he could convert his predicament into a special adventure.

So down the Missouri floated the two flatboats, heaped high with the spoils of the two-year sporting expedition, as Bridger and Gore led the horse party up the Little Missouri River toward the Black Hills. For good reason the area remained "uncharted" on contemporary maps: hostile Teton Sioux controlled the country, and parties that embarked for the Hills seldom returned. Primeau and local Assiniboine leaders had advised against the excursion, but Gore was determined and Bridger was unafraid. For two weeks the pack train pushed up the Little Missouri River, into the badlands and across the Belle Fourche River.

No luxuries for the aristocrat on this trip! Gore slept in buffalo robes on the ground, ate in the general mess, and filled a turn on night guard duty. Still, opportunities existed in route for the shoot-ing of numerous bison, elk, deer, antelope, and bear. Gore would not be denied.

Despite the ominous warnings they had received, Gore's men sighted no Sioux Indians until they had penetrated well into the Black Hills. Then, suddenly, a war party of about 180 men, led by Bear's Rib, surrounded them. It had been the Sioux leader's practice to slay whites who straggled into the sacred Black Hills, but this time he relented. He offered an ultimatum: Gore and his men could stand

and fight, outnumbered ten to one, or they could abandon their horses, weapons, equipment, and clothes and walk out the way they had come in. Even to the headstrong baronet, the choice was obvious.

The eighteen naked men and their hounds spent almost five weeks retracing the three hundred miles back to the mouth of the Little Missouri River. They usually traveled at night, because they were defenseless if they encountered any band of hostile warriors. The men survived on wild roots, berries, and whatever rabbits the hounds could catch. Near the mouth of the Little Missouri, the bedraggled company met a band of friendly Hidatsa Indians, who fed them and led them downriver to their camp near Fort Berthold. By then it was the end of October 1856, the same time of year that the English gentry assembled to hunt stags in Scotland.

Each November, just before the ice set in, Joseph Picotte's "Opposition" fur operation sent a mackinaw boat down the Missouri River to collect furs from its posts and to carry to St. Louis messages and supply requisitions for the following season. Gore arranged for Bridger and eleven other members of his ill-fated group to return to Missouri on this boat. He paid the men in improvised vouchers drawn on the "Opposition" company, redeemable in St. Louis through Baring Brothers/London. Bridger would instruct the crews on the two flatboats—still waiting at the mouth of the Cheyenne River—to proceed to St. Louis, and he would supervise the storage of Gore's spoils.

Sir St. George Gore, his two servants, and three other members of his original retinue accepted the offer of the Hidatsa leader Crow's Breast. They would spend the winter in an earthen lodge at Like-A-Fishhook village, near Fort Berthold. Stripped of all the luxuries with which he had entered the American prairies, the aristocrat passed these snowy, windswept months in the style of a Hidatsa. Surely, during some of those frigid nights, he recalled classical Greek tragedies and compared their heroes' woes to his experiences in the West.

In July 1857, a buckskin-clad Gore and his two servants boarded the steamboat *Twilight* at Fort Berthold and descended the Missouri

River. They spent the remainder of the summer in St. Louis, lodged in the exquisite Planter's House. They then embarked for New York City and England, with the pack of hounds. One year late, the aristocrat reached home in time to join the annual fall stag hunt in the Scottish Highlands.

Gore would return to America only once again, making a trip to the Florida Everglades in 1876, two years before his death. The baronet never married and, when he died, at age sixty-seven, his title devolved on his cousin, who became the ninth baronet of Manor Gore. In 1878 relatives interred Sir St. George Gore in the family vault at the Old Parish Church of St. Andrew in Hove, Sussex County, England.

The sporting foray of Gore into the American West—and specifically into Montana—marked one of the region's first, most lavishly supplied and organized expeditions arranged solely for the purpose of hunting and fishing. To Gore, expense was no issue—he spent more than $250,000 on the three-year trip. What mattered was the chase. After that came the kill, and the most important factor of all—the style one maintained while pursuing one's quarry.

On the first two counts, the baronet emerged victorious: his party shot an estimated 4,000 bison, 1,500 elk, 2,000 deer, 1,500 antelope, 500 bear, and scores of other assorted game animals. On the lifestyle count, however, Gore proved less triumphant. The prairie wilderness successfully reduced the aristocratic sportsman from his accustomed level of incredible luxury to one of mere survival. Ultimately, this paragon of the out-of-state hunter was lucky to escape with his life.

CHAPTER 2

THE THOMAS TRAGEDY ON
THE YELLOWSTONE

In December 1864, seven-year-old Homer Thomas sat down with mother at the kitchen table to compose a letter to his grandmother. It would be his first Christmas separated from the large Thomas clan in Illinois, just across the Mississippi River from St. Louis. The preceding May, George Thomas, his wife Lucy, and their two small sons had left their farm near Shiloh, Illinois, to travel nearly five months by ox train across the Great Plains. The Thomases settled on a ranch in the Gallatin Valley, near present-day Manhattan, in October 1864. George rapidly built a cottonwood-log house for their first winter in the fledgling Montana Territory.

Although the frontier ranch offered a seven-year-old boy many diversions, the thought of Christmas rendered him homesick for the prosperous farms of western Illinois. With his mother's coaching, Homer's descriptions to his grandmother reveal that longing in them both.

Dear Grandma:

I thought you would like to hear from us all, so I thought I would write you a few lines to let you know that I have not forgotten you all yet, even if I am away out here in the Indian and gold country.

There is plenty of gold out here, especially in Virginia City, but it is hard to get hold of it. . . .

I wish that I was back there to get some of your good things to eat, like apples and cider. There is not any out here in this mountain country. Still, I have had some nice antelope, deer, and elk meat. I think elk is the best of all. And there is some big bears out here too. We have not killed any yet, but some of the hunters kill them. . . .

Grandma, you come out here to visit us, and you see how you would like this country. There is plenty of big mountains around us, about eight or ten miles on either side of us. On the mountains there is bully pine timber. Father took our team and went up there and got two big loads of nice poles to build fence for a cattle yard. We have plenty of wood right close to home, but it is all cottonwood, Balm of Gilead, and willow.

With a child's logic—possibly influenced by his parents' remarks—Homer also revealed his expectations for Christmas in Montana:

Well, Grandma, it is pretty near Christmas time, and I do not expect to get many things this year. For it is not like home, because old Santa Claus do not come out here to give children things, because he thinks all of the children are too smart to come to this old place.

The letter to Isabella and John Thomas in Belleville, Illinois, brought these grandparents much holiday joy. When the Thomases' other nine children and their families arrived at the farmhouse during the Yule season, John read the letter aloud and others reread it silently, by kerosene lamp. To one of George Thomas's older brothers—William K. Thomas—the child's words struck a particularly responsive chord.

Bill Thomas had suffered devastating personal losses during 1864. First, both of his infant twin girls had died of pneumonia. Then, within weeks, his young wife had succumbed to the illness. At age thirty-four, Bill Thomas was left with a six-year-old son, a prosperous farm, increasing rheumatism in his hips, and a life in shambles. The

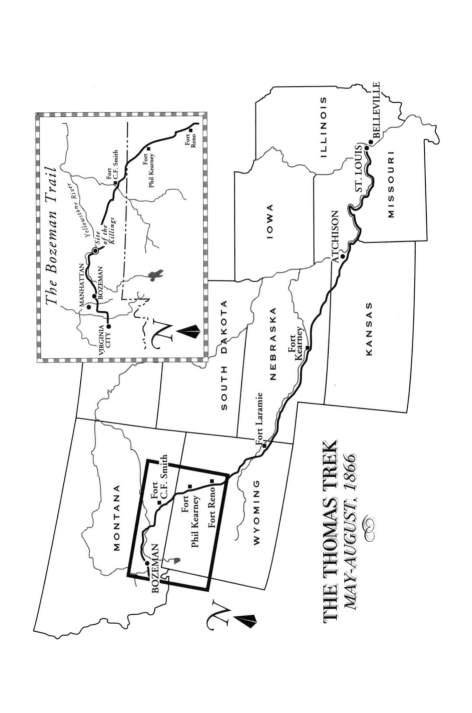

The Bozeman Trail

VIRGINIA
CITY
MANHATTAN
BOZEMAN
Yellowstone River
Site
of the
Killings
Fort
C.F. Smith
Fort
Phil Kearney
Fort
Reno

N

ILLINOIS
BELLEVILLE
ST. LOUIS
MISSOURI
ATCHISON
IOWA
KANSAS
NEBRASKA
Fort
Kearney
SOUTH DAKOTA
Fort Laramie
WYOMING
MONTANA
Fort
C.F. Smith
Fort
Phil Kearney
Fort Reno
BOZEMAN

N

THE THOMAS TREK
MAY-AUGUST, 1866

idea of a fresh start in Montana Territory offered real possibilities.

By the autumn of 1865, Bill Thomas had determined his course. He would leave his farm, which harbored so many wrenching memories, and cross the Great Plains by wagon to settle near his brother, under the Gallatin Valley's big sky. So he purchased a $500 pair of mules and a "prairie schooner"—a relatively light, narrow freight wagon, its hoops covered in canvas, developed in the 1850s, for one-way family travel on the Great Plains.

By May 1866, Bill Thomas had transferred his farm to the family to operate, packed his household possessions and overland supplies in the schooner, and headed west. Thomas's party consisted of his seven-year-old son Charles and Joseph Schultz. Schultz was a thirty-five-year-old Canadian who had worked on the Thomas farm for several years. He showed a special talent for handling mules and wanted to try his luck in the Montana placer-gold diggings.

The first leg of the trek to Montana was the short jaunt from Belleville to the steamboat levee at St. Louis. Here Thomas contracted space on the Missouri River steamboat *Paragon*. Four days later, the boat arrived in Atchison, Kansas. Camped at Atchison—a popular terminus for the Oregon Trail in 1866—Bill Thomas wrote to his parents in Illinois:

> Charley stands the trip well. He was all over, and through, and on top of the boat. And camp life seems to suit him. He takes hold of camp duties with delight and does more than his part. Not one word of complaint or dissatisfaction has come from his mouth.
>
> Single wagons and trains leave here daily, loaded down with goods and provisions for different parts of the mining country, besides a daily line of coaches leaving for Denver City. . . . We have not connected ourselves with any train, as it is not considered dangerous to travel alone from here to Fort Kearney [Nebraska Territory], which is about 250 miles from here. . . . But I have been informed that we will have to go under military rules and regulations from Fort Kearney.

Indian-white conflicts on the northern Great Plains in the mid-1860s had forced the use of military escorts for civilian immigrants and contract freighters. Following a Sioux uprising in Minnesota, bands of eastern Sioux retreated westward and united with the Northern Cheyenne. Together the tribes challenged the whites who penetrated their declared bison-hunting lands. The most successful Indian tactic involved attacking any vulnerable white party traveling within the claimed lands and killing its members.

The Bozeman Trail offered a case in point, since it ran right through the middle of these traditional hunting grounds, encompassing the Powder, the Tongue, and the Big Horn River drainages. In 1866 the Sioux leader Red Cloud justifiably mistrusted white intentions for this region. Even as U.S. Army Colonel Henry B. Carrington participated in a treaty conference at Fort Laramie (in present-day Wyoming), he was directing the construction of three military posts along the Bozeman Trail—smack in the heart of Sioux and Cheyenne country.

When the Thomas party pulled out of Atchison on May 28, Bill Thomas recognized the potential danger. Because of its excellent mule team and a cargo of only eighteen hundred pounds, the schooner traveled the 250 miles to Fort Kearney, on the Platte River, in fewer than ten days. Here, on June 12, Bill Thomas attached his wagon to Hugh Kirkendall's mule train of forty wagons for protection from rumored Indian raiders on the North Platte River route to Fort Laramie. Although this 335-mile leg of the trek proved uneventful, the train's slower pace meant that the travelers did not reach Fort Laramie until July 5, 1866.

Following only a one-day rest, the Thomas party rejoined Kirkendall's mule train—to which was added two private wagons and another thirty-wagon ox team led by Thomas Dillon—to push into hostile Sioux country. Crossing the North Platte River at Bridger's Ferry, the convoy plodded up the Bozeman Trail toward the newly constructed Fort Reno.

Although the Thomases and Joe Schultz caught glimpses of raiding parties at a distance, the size of their combined train discouraged any direct attacks. More aggravating to the impatient Thomas became the constant dust, heat, and slow pace: It took better than two weeks to cover the 170 miles between Fort Laramie and Fort Reno.

Both the soldiers and the civilians at Fort Reno advised that any travel farther north on the Bozeman Trail would be extremely dangerous, except in large parties. Because most of the grass around the fort had been grazed, the Kirkendall–Dillon–Thomas train moved north of the post and camped on the Crazy Woman's Fork of the Powder River to await additional wagons. Ever so slowly, Thomas's impatience to reach the Gallatin Valley became tempered with realism. In his diary for July 22-23, he noted:

> Soon after camping, four Indians were seen lurking around the herd. They raised quite an excitement among the boys. They were fired on and were last seen making their way across the hills. . . . This is a dangerous place to camp on account of the Indians. Two men were killed here a few days ago by Indians. We had expected an attack here, but no Indians to be seen.

On July 23, a hundred-wagon federal-government supply train, under full military escort, reached the Thomas camp. With these reinforcements, the Kirkendall–Dillon–Thomas party embarked on July 24 to skirt northeast of the Bighorn Mountains and cover the remaining fifty miles to the new Fort Phil Kearney. Still, from the events of that day, Bill Thomas might have learned the lesson of safety in numbers:

> Left camp at 5 a.m. The Government train goes ahead, and the three citizens' wagons (including mine) follow after it. The Dillon ox train of thirty wagons is next, and Kirkendall's forty-wagon mule train follows in the rear. The government train and our group reached Clear

Creek at about 2 p.m., but the ox train stopped three miles back and was attacked by Indians. Not much damage was done, though—one mule was killed and one mule wounded.

The worst fight involved the five men Wagon master Dillon led back to see what had detained Kirkendall. When within a quarter mile of Kirkendall's train, they were surrounded by twenty-five Indians. After fighting four or five hours, they reached the train, killing two Indians and carrying Dillon, who was mortally wounded. Kirkendall's train then moved up to the ox train, where they corralled for the night.

July 25: Wagon master Dillon, who was wounded yesterday, died last night.

The reunited convoy rolled into Fort Phil Kearney, where friends buried Thomas Dillon on July 26. By that time, the threat of Sioux attacks had become so great that Colonel Carrington, commanding officer at the fort, forbade any wagons to leave the post until he could provide additional military protection. As the days dragged on, Bill Thomas became more and more impatient to retake the Bozeman Trail. Yet daily reports of Sioux depredations returned him to reality:

Fort Philip Kearney is the most beautiful place for a fort that I have seen west of Fort Leavenworth [Kansas]. Its mountain scenery is most striking and majestic, with its beautiful range of hills on either side, north and south—as if they were throwing their arms around and clasping one in their bosom. . . . For a moment I stand gazing at the lofty peaks, now at the rugged rocks, while my mind runs over the wild scenes of nature that spread out before my eyes.

I am meditating upon the adventure that I am about to take, counting the cost, summing up the danger. Cold chills run through my body.

Bill Thomas's diary entry is prophetic, revealing an American West that he had never conceived from the safe, lush cropland of Illinois. And a larger West, too—Thomas remained more than 275 miles from the Gallatin Valley and his brother.

Finally, on August 2, the Thomas party and a caravan of 112 wagons trailed out of Fort Phil Kearney. On the next day, this convoy was overtaken by a government train of forty wagons and two companies of U.S. Army infantry, guided by the legendary sixty-two-year-old mountain man Jim Bridger. Thomas did not underestimate the security offered by the increased numbers and by the military contingent, but the train's slow pace continued to frustrate him.

The Bozeman Trail between Fort Phil Kearney and the site for the new Fort C. F. Smith on the Bighorn River wound for seventy miles over the foothills of the Bighorn Mountains. Thomas remarked on the beauty of the rolling grasslands, but he could not forget the danger such country also held:

About a half mile's drive from camp this morning, on the hillside to the left of the road, is a grave containing the bodies of five men who were killed a few days ago by the Indians. As I passed by the grave, I saw that the wolves had made an opening to the inmates and had torn the flesh from the bodies and left their ribs exposed. Such is the haste and the depravity of man out here that he will hardly take the time to pay his last respects to the dead—but leaves them for the wild beast of the field to cry and howl over, and often feast upon. . . .

Just before we crossed a small creek [two days later], we saw a lone grave to the left of the road. Its inmate was deposited there in July of last year, but we could not make out his name, since part of the head-board was gone. He had left Chambersburg, Pennsylvania, on May 8, 1865, and was killed here by Indians.

The poor fellow's remains had not been left in peace to molder away into dust—but, as his life had been taken by the merciless Savages, so had his body been disturbed by the wild and unsatiated wolves. They had dug down until they had left the inmate half uncovered and knawed the flesh from his face. We could see that he had been scalped: a sad plight to look at, but a worse one to reflect upon.

After eight days on the Bozeman Trail, Jim Bridger guided the large wagon train to the Bighorn River. Here the federal government contingent fell out, to begin construction of Fort C. F. Smith. The reconstituted train that approached the Bighorn River ford consisted of the Thomas party, two other private mule teams, the Kirkendall train of forty wagons, and the Dillon ox train of thirty wagons. Bridger assured the civilians that they had passed through the dangerous Sioux-controlled country and that they had reached the domain of the Crows, a tribe generally friendly to whites. So Bill Thomas's fear of an attack by marauding warriors diminished. In any event, reports said that another train of several hundred wagons followed them by just a few days.

Even in mid-August, the crossing of the Bighorn River proved difficult. Bill Thomas recounted:

Quite a sad accident happened today. Three of the men belonging to the [Kirkendall] train, while crossing the river in search of a better ford, had their horses pitch into a deep hole. They were thrown from their horses, which were struggling for shore. Two of the men got out by grabbing their horses by the tails and being dragged.

When they were out, they ran to the assistance of their comrade— who was swimming down the torrent and in need of help. But, before they could reach him, he sank and was seen no more—until three or four hours later, when his lifeless body was taken from the stream.

Our wagon and the two other citizens' wagons were all landed safely. But in swimming the mules over, three mules were drowned (none of ours). The ox wagons are just now crossing, but several head of their cattle drowned while being driven across.

The Bozeman Trail west of Fort C. F. Smith wound over hills and through valleys for about 140 miles before striking the Yellowstone River west of present-day Reedpoint. The route then hugged the Yellowstone, crossing to the north side just west of Big Timber, and ran over Bozeman Pass to the Gallatin Valley, and on to Virginia City.

For a couple of days, Thomas found the trail through southern Montana's virgin grasslands—up over ridge divides and down through creek valleys—relaxing, particularly after a month under the constant threat of Sioux attack. Yet the slow pace of the ox train continued to bother him. He and Charley and Joe Schultz now were traveling in safe Crow country, and their Gallatin Valley destination beckoned. On August 17, when further delays seemed evident, Bill Thomas reached a decision:

> Friday morning the train started out at about six o'clock. One of the freight wagons broke down about an hour after leaving camp. My wagon and the two other private wagons passed the train and went together for two or three miles. Then the other two wagons stopped behind me, thinking it safer to wait for the train.
>
> I determined, trusting in the Lord, to go ahead. We nooned on Beavais Creek, about ten miles from where we left the train, and then we drove about eight miles in the afternoon. Saw plenty of antelope and buffalo.

In fact, the next five days became almost idyllic for the Thomas party. They finally had escaped the restraints and routines of an organized wagon train, and had begun to make good time. The travelers saw no Indians or Indian sign. In each of the little creek valleys, they found herds of bison and antelope and, once, some grizzly sign. At evening campsites, they gathered berries and currants. At one campsite, west of their crossing of the Clarks Fork of the Yellowstone, they even engaged in a diversion:

> *August 21:* . . . About forty rods to the right of us, in a little ravine, under some willow trees, I found a spring of the best water I ever drank of. Charley and I spent a half day cleaning it out and nicely

walling it up. We made a very nice job of it. We called it "Thomas Spring."

On the next day, the lone wagon forded the Stillwater River and followed the Bozeman Trail ruts as they meandered down from the hills to the Yellowstone River bottom. Here they passed the point where the Bridger Cutoff Trail struck the Bozeman Trail. Bill Thomas wrote in his diary that evening.

> In the afternoon we drove five miles and crossed a river [Bridger Creek]. While crossing it we lost our coffee pot. Drove three miles from there and camped for the night on a nice little branch, a few hundred yards upslope from the Yellowstone.
> Broke our champagne bottle.

Those words constitute the last entry in Bill Thomas's small, brown leather pocket diary. The Thomas party's overland trip from Illinois to the Gallatin Valley ended there—on the south bank of the Yellowstone River, less than one mile east of the Greycliff promontory. On the evening of August 23, a band of at least twenty Sioux warriors attacked and killed the Thomas party.

That site currently is marked by a Montana Department of Transportation sign, erected on a narrow, grassy strip between Interstate 90 and the frontage road (old U.S. Highway 10). Behind the sign rests the common grave of Bill Thomas, seven-year-old Charley, and Joe Schultz.

During the morning of August 24, a wagon driven by S. H. Murray—running ahead of the thirty-wagon train led by Captain John S. Waller—discovered the tragedy. The campfire still smoldered, and the Sioux had ransacked the schooner. Its contents had been burned, carried off, or scattered across the prairie. The prized mules and Joe Schultz were nowhere in sight. Bill Thomas's body lay beside the large rear wheels of the wagon, with thirteen arrows in it. Murray found Charley's slight body near the front wheels, carrying three arrows. Both had been scalped; the blood remained fresh.

The Sioux had planted two-foot sticks with strips of coarse, blue-green cloth tied to their tops around the bodies of the father and son. Although the Murray party feared the return of the raiders, they gathered some of the family's remaining possessions: a few books; the family Bible; Charley's hunting knife; one of his boots; Bill Thomas's diary. Murray's group then spent a long, terrifying night on constant guard, awaiting the arrival of the Waller train.

The morning of August 25 brought the Waller wagons to the scene. Members of the train discovered the body of Joe Schultz, scalped and punctured by a dozen arrows, lying on the bank of the Yellowstone River, downslope from the Thomas campsite. He had been fishing when the surprise attack began; he had caught two Yellowstone cutthroat trout. Several men hastily dug a shallow grave and buried the three bodies, while others scanned the wooded river bottom, the bluffs, and the grassy hills for Sioux. The immigrants quickly lettered headboards and erected them to mark the common grave.

Captain Waller delivered the news of the tragedy and the family's effects—including the schooner, the diary, the Sioux marking sticks, and many of the arrows—to George Thomas, Bill's brother who lived in the Gallatin Valley. This time, it was not little Homer Thomas who wrote to his grandmother; his father assumed that onerous task. In his September 1866, letter to the family in Belleville, Illinois, George explained:

> Bill was very anxious to reach the Gallatin, and it was generally supposed that they were safe from Indian attack, as they were in Crow country—the Crows being at peace with the whites. Old Jim Bridger was with the big wagon train, and he conveyed that idea throughout the camp. But it proved a sad mistake, for the Sioux have had easy access into Crow country and have committed many depredations there in the past two years.

This explanation must have rung hollow to the Thomases, from whom their son and grandson had departed just four months earlier.

This tragic killing might have been lost to history were it not for Bill Thomas's nephew, John T. Lienesch of O'Fallon, Illinois. In 1937, Lienesch retraced his uncle's 1866 trail west, armed with Bill Thomas's letters and diary. After much investigation, he located the gravesite east of the town of Greycliff. With the help of Robert Fletcher of the Montana Department of Highways, Lienesch worked to erect a roadside historical sign marking this grave and commemorating the many overland immigrants who never reached their destinations.

Today the Thomas–Schultz grave seems incongruous, sandwiched in the midst of the Yellowstone power corridor. Interstate 90 runs four lanes of whizzing traffic within yards of the gravesite on one side, while old U.S. Highway 10 passes just as closely on the other side. North toward the Yellowstone River—where Joe Schultz was fishing—are parallel tracks of Montana Rail Link trains (formerly the Northern Pacific Railroad), power lines, telephone wires, and underground pipelines. Such is the layering of people, events, and structures on the Montana landscape.

On your next headlong rush down I-90, zipping between Greycliff and Reedpoint, stop to locate the roadside sign beyond the highway's frontage fence. It is worth reflecting on the adventure that Bill Thomas, little Charley Thomas, and Joe Schultz undertook in the summer of 1866, since their final resting place sits right in the midst of the symbols of modern Montana. The gravesite proves we are not far removed from our history—in time, in place, and in emotion.

CHAPTER 3

THE MASSACRE ON THE MARIAS

When two cultures clash, the outcome can be horrific. Antagonism and violence often dominate accommodation and compromise. The land that Montana now comprises became a battlefield for just such a cultural conflict during the last half of the nineteenth century. When settlers arrived in country that had been the centuries-long domain of several American Indian tribes, discord inevitably resulted. In Montana the clash of cultural systems proved relatively short-lived because the combatants were mismatched. But today the results of that conflict still define, and even haunt, the relationship between American Indians and whites in the state.

A case in point is the contentious relationship that developed in the 1860s between advancing settlers and the three factions of the Blackfeet Confederacy, which included the Pikuni (Piegan), the Kainah (Bloods), and the Siksika (Northern Blackfeet/Blackfeet proper). These tribes remained politically independent, but their members spoke a common language and shared many customs; they intermarried and united in war against common foes.

Blackfeet culture involved an intense, pervasive spiritual relationship between the individual and his or her environment, and the white concept of land ownership was viewed as irrelevant at best. For the sake of survival, the tribes split into numerous bands—each with its own leader—and moved camp seasonally, in response to migrating bison herds and weather conditions. These bands would reunite to perform rituals, such as the summer Sun Dance ceremony, and to launch war parties. A Blackfeet man could gain honor and wealth in warfare against tribal enemies, or by stealing horses from traditional foes.

By 1850 the Blackfeet—with a population estimated at eight thousand—effectively controlled a bison-rich domain that stretched from the Rocky Mountains east to the Bears Paw Mountains, and from the North Saskatchewan River south to the headwaters of the Missouri River. The area was twice the size of New England, and aggressive protection of this land had earned the Blackfeet a reputation as the fiercest warriors on the northern Great Plains. That reputation had spread after the combative encounter of July 27, 1806, when explorer Meriwether Lewis and three of his men fought eight Pikuni hunters on the Two Medicine River.

Despite such fights, Blackfeet bands traded in relative peace with agents of the Hudson's Bay Company, the Northwest Fur Company, and the American Fur Company through the first half of the nineteenth century. A harbinger of change came in 1855. The federal government designed Lame Bull's Treaty to impose peace and order among tribes both east and west of the Northern Rockies. This agreement eroded Blackfeet superiority, however, since it created a "legal" Blackfeet domain that extended only from the Rocky Mountains east to the mouth of the Milk River and from the Canadian border south to the Three Forks and the Musselshell River. The government established its first Blackfeet Agency at Fort Benton in that same year.

When prospectors discovered placer gold at Bannack in July 1862, the resulting flood of miners constituted the first real wave of white settlement into what would become Montana Territory. Subsequent strikes throughout the Montana Rockies drew more white miners, settlers, and merchants. These immigrants penetrated Blackfeet lands,

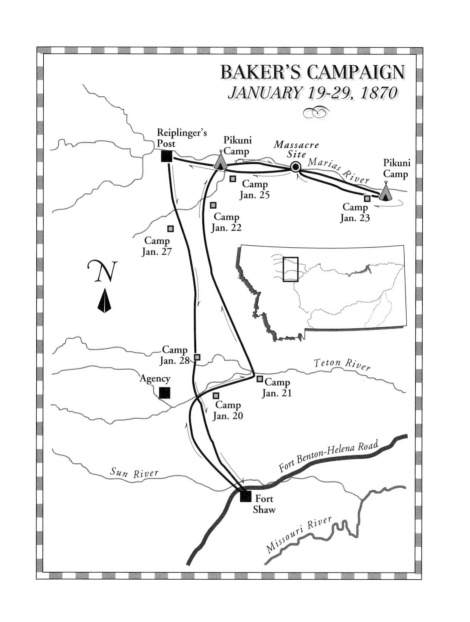

particularly at Fort Benton and along the roads that radiated from that river port. The Blackfeet reaction to this white invasion of their hunting grounds took swift and often violent form. War parties of young men attacked small, white prospecting parties and ran off the miners' and ranchers' livestock. Simultaneously white fur traders continued to ply the Blackfeet with alcohol and trade goods to increase their production of buffalo robes—at the expense of their vital bison herds. The cultural stability that the Blackfeet had developed prior to 1862 began to deteriorate.

The influence of the federal military in Montana had been nominal until 1866, mostly because of the Civil War. Once the War Between the States was over, the federal government responded to white Montanans' pleas for protection along transportation routes to their placer strikes and isolated agricultural valleys. The government built Camp Cooke near the confluence of the Judith and Missouri Rivers in 1866. The next year, soldiers constructed Fort Shaw on the Sun River, within the Blackfeet reserve. Troops from Fort Shaw's four-hundred-man garrison regularly protected travelers and freighters along the heavily used Fort Benton-to-Helena portion of the Mullan Road.

Federal agents in 1865 also had negotiated a treaty with Blackfeet leaders. In return for an annual distribution of goods valued at $50,000, an annuity to be granted for the next twenty years, the Indians agreed to pull back the southern boundary of their reservation. The reserve area shrunk, its edge holding to a line running down the Teton and Missouri Rivers to the mouth of the Milk River. But the treaty was never ratified, leaving the Blackfeet puzzled by a white political system that made an agreement but really did not make an agreement. When the Blackfeet received no annuity goods, they believed that they had been betrayed—particularly since whites had settled throughout their former land between the Teton-Missouri and Musselshell Rivers. The imminent clash of cultures became more and more evident.

Just as the Blackfeet remained factionalized into small bands with multiple leaders, the white political system that had developed to deal with Western Indians also functioned in overlapping jurisdictions. Only the U.S. Senate could make treaties with individual tribes, which it considered autonomous political entities like foreign governments. The War Department held the responsibility for protecting U.S. citizens and their property. The Office of Indian Affairs administered the Indian programs, treating the people as federal wards, through the civilian-dominated Department of the Interior. This complicated pattern of jurisdiction became even more confused by the Department of the Interior's tendency to appoint military officers as reservation agents in the post-Civil War period.

Between 1862 and 1869, a cyclical sequence of Blackfeet-white action and reaction developed in Montana Territory. As the Indians' lifestyle disintegrated in the face of a white invasion, smallpox, and alcohol, Blackfeet chiefs lost control of their young warriors. These young men attacked prospecting parties and isolated ranches. They killed white settlers and stole their horses and mules, to sell them in Canada for alcohol, repeating rifles, and ammunition. Whites, in the vigilante tradition, shot and hanged random Indians who often played no part in the immediate depredations. At the same time, they exaggerated the Blackfeet threat in their camp meetings, newspapers, and legislative memorials to the U.S. Congress. Cause-and-effect justifications became obscured as the violent confrontation of the two cultures gained a sporadic, disjointed life of its own.

The pivotal incident in this sequence involved the killing of Malcolm Clarke on the night of August 17, 1869. Clarke had been dismissed from West Point in the mid-1830s because of his pugnacious character. By 1839 he had begun trading for the American Fur Company on the upper Missouri, where he cultivated unusually strong ties with the Pikuni tribe of the Blackfeet. Clarke quickly rose to the position of the company's main buffalo-robe trader in the Marias drainage. He married Cutting-Off-Head-Woman, daughter of a sub-chief in Mountain Chief's Pikuni band, who bore him several children. During the 1840s and 1850s, Clarke gained the trust and respect of many Blackfeet leaders, despite his hot temper. They conferred on him the name "Four Bears," because of his prowess in killing grizzlies.

With the liquidation of the American Fur Company in 1864, the Clarke family established a ranch on Little Prickly Pear Creek, about twenty-five miles north of the mining town of Helena. In addition to raising livestock, Clarke's prosperous ranch served as a regular stop on the Fort Benton-Helena road. Many immigrants who had disembarked from steamboats at Fort Benton enroute to the placer mines became the recipients of Clarke's hospitality. His reputation grew as one of the fledgling territory's prominent citizens.

At the Clarke ranch in 1867, a cousin of Cutting-Off-Head-Woman, Owl Child, precipitated an ugly but seemingly inconsequential event. Owl Child was the son of Mountain Chief, but he had married into the Heavy Runner band of the Pikuni. The young man grew into a fierce warrior and a fearless horse thief, but his rash actions had forced his banishment from Heavy Runner's band. He had been branded a renegade by the Blackfeet and had returned to his father's band, where Mountain Chief protected him.

In 1867 Owl Child visited his cousin at the Clarke ranch in Malcolm Clarke's absence. During the visit, someone stole Owl Child's horses. He had not recovered them by the time of his departure, so he appropriated several of Clarke's horses to ride home. He also took Clarke's prized spyglass.

Clarke discovered the theft when he returned home. With Horace, his fifteen-year-old son, Clarke trailed Owl Child to Mountain Chief's village. There he openly berated Owl Child, Horace struck him, and the Clarkes recovered their stolen property. Only Clarke's longtime friendship with the Pikuni prevented retaliation and permitted their safe return to the Clarke ranch. Owl Child's honor had been challenged, however, and he vowed revenge on Four Bears.

Two years later, on the evening of August 17, 1869, Owl Child again visited his cousin at the Clarke ranch. This time he came in the company of four other Pikuni, including Black Weasel, another son of Mountain Chief. Owl Child appeared friendly and conciliatory, and apparently the earlier incident had been forgotten by both parties. After midnight, under the guise of checking some horses, the Pikuni lured Horace Clarke from the ranchhouse. Near the corrals, Bear Chief shot Horace through the face. Horace fell to the ground, severely wounded but not dead.

Upon hearing the shot, Malcolm Clarke and Owl Child rushed from the house. A man named Eagle Rib shot Clarke at point-blank range, and Owl Child slashed Clarke's forehead with a hatchet. The victim died instantly. Cutting-Off-Head-Woman's blood relationship to the attackers may have been the only thing that prevented her death and that of her children.

Cutting-Off-Head-Woman and her daughters nursed Horace Clarke back to health, but the real damage had been done. Whites interpreted the event as the wanton slaying of a legendary Montanan by a band of marauding Pikuni—although it was closer to a family dispute. The killing of Malcolm Clarke produced public furor, which would eventually have dire results for all of the Pikuni.

Amid the public frenzy generated by the Clarke killing, U.S. Marshal William F. Wheeler of Helena prepared an indictment for consideration by the grand jury. In it he pled the settlers' case against marauding Blackfeet and urgently requested the federal government's protection in this clash of cultures. The *Helena Weekly Herald* reported Wheeler's plea:

[There] is a declaration of war on the whites of Montana, and some measure should be adopted to meet the emergency. . . . Ours is the contest between civilization and barbarism, and we must risk our lives and sacrifice our hard-earned property to defend [that civilization], unless the general government gives us the means of defense. To this we are entitled, as we left homes of comfort in the East to plant civilization in the wilderness.

On October 9, 1869, the grand jury issued warrants for the arrest of Owl Child, Eagle Rib, Bear Chief, Black Weasel, and Black Bear—all aligned with Mountain Chief's band of Pikuni.

Wheeler first delivered the indictment and warrants to Brevet Brigadier General Alfred H. Sully, an Army officer serving as superintendent of Indian Affairs for Montana Territory, stationed in Helena. The excitable Sully endorsed some type of limited military action against the Pikuni and sent Wheeler's request for federal protection to his superior, the commissioner of Indian Affairs in Washington, D.C. Sully also forwarded a copy to Lieutenant General Philip H. Sheridan, the commander of the Army's Military Division of the Missouri (including Montana Territory), stationed in Chicago, Illinois.

When Wheeler received no immediate response, he carried a copy of the indictment and the warrants to Brevet Brigadier General Philippe Regis de Trobriand, the commander of military affairs for Montana Territory, at Fort Shaw. De Trobriand, somewhat removed from the public frenzy swirling around the mining camps, perceived the Blackfeet-white situation in less dire terms. When he directed Wheeler's request to his superior, General Sheridan, de Trobriand referred to an early 1869 communiqué he had sent to the general. It said,

> The Blackfeet [Siksika], the Pend d'Oreilles, the Bloods [Kainah], and even part of the Piegans [Pikuni], remain perfectly quiet, protesting that they have nothing to do with these attacks on the persons or properties of white men. . . . The responsibility of the recent hostilities and depredations seems, therefore, to rest exclusively on one band of Piegans [Mountain Chief's Pikuni] and on some roaming vagabonds of different tribes, acting on their own hook and independent of their own people, as is often the case in Indian country. This [threat] is not alto-

gether very formidable . . . and I do not much believe in the genuineness of the fear expressed by the settlers.

During the autumn of 1869, General Sheridan remained puzzled over the conflicting reports on the Blackfeet threat. Sheridan, long a champion of aggressive action against hostile Indians, remained uncharacteristically calm. Still, as early as October 21, he requested permission from the general of the U.S. Army, William Tecumseh Sherman, for a possible campaign.

> I think it would be the best plan to let me find out exactly where these Indians are going to spend the winter and, about the time of a good heavy snow, I will send out a party and try to strike them. About the 15th of January, they will be very helpless and . . . to simply keep the troops on the defensive will not stop the murders. We must occasionally strike where it hurts. . . .

With Sherman's approval of his request, General Sheridan again tried to appraise the situation in Montana Territory. General Sully, in Helena, continued to recommend military action against the Pikuni. General de Trobriand, at Fort Shaw, again counseled restraint:

> Those who are known or suspected to be hostile are scattered along or beyond the frontier line [the Canadian border]. . . . At the first move, they would disappear in the British Territory. . . . Those offending parties are either with Mountain Chief or Bear Chief, and number but a few lodges in each band. . . .
>
> In conclusion, I do not see, so far, an opportunity for striking a successful blow. The only Indians within reach are decidedly friendly, and nothing would be worse, I think, than to chastise them for offenses of which they are not guilty. I speak not only with a view to justice and humanity, but for the best interest of the Territory.

As a result of this confusion, General Sheridan directed Sully to meet with the pertinent Blackfeet leaders. He ordered Sully to demand that they return all the stolen livestock the tribe held and that they produce the five renegades named in Marshal Wheeler's warrants. He then detailed his trusted aide, Inspector General James Allen Hardie, to Montana to assess the situation firsthand. Brevet Major General Hardie departed Chicago on December 29, 1869, and arrived in Corinne, Utah Territory, via the Union Pacific Railroad. From there he took a stagecoach, which reached Helena on January 5, 1870, and Fort Shaw on January 7.

At the outpost, General Sully reported to Hardie concerning his January 1 meeting with four friendly chiefs at the Blackfeet Agency: the Pikuni leaders Heavy Runner, Little Wolf, and Big Lake and the Kainah headman Gray Eyes. Sully had given these principals two weeks to accomplish their tasks, after which he threatened, "The government, tired out with the repeated aggressions by their people, was determined to send troops to make war against them, as the only way to protect the lives and property of the whites."

In contrast to his earlier recommendations, General Sully suggested a more moderate plan to Hardie: that several Pikuni chiefs be captured and held hostage until the other Pikuni delivered the renegades. Equally surprising to Hardie, General de Trobriand changed his position and now strongly endorsed a military attack on selected bands of the Pikuni.

De Trobriand's scouts reported that Mountain Chief's band had returned from Canada and had established winter camp on the Marias River—well within the range of troops stationed at Fort Shaw. General Hardie immediately detailed the fort's civilian interpreter/scout Joe Kipp to the Marias to pinpoint the locations of the camps along the river. Kipp returned on January 12 with the report that Mountain Chief's band had encamped in "the Big Bend of the Marias" and that Bear Chief's camp sat several miles upstream. Other Pikuni had settled into camps at intervals on the Marias, all the way upstream to

Reiplinger's Northwest Fur Company post near Willow Rounds. Kipp assured General Hardie that, should he accompany an expedition to the Marias, he could distinguish between the friendly and the hostile Pikuni camps.

Late in December, General de Trobriand ordered Brevet Colonel Eugene M. Baker, commander of the Second U.S. Cavalry, stationed at Fort Ellis (near Bozeman), to report to Fort Shaw with four companies of men. This order had been issued prior to the arrival at Fort Shaw of General Hardie, just in case his superiors approved a military action. Baker and his 210 mounted men arrived at the outpost on January 14, after covering almost 190 miles in severe winter weather.

On the preceding day, Hardie had telegraphed a brief report on the Montana situation to General Phil Sheridan in Chicago. It concluded,

> The question is, whether the principal design [of a military move-ment] should be the chastisement of the Indians or the capture of them for hostages. The practical result of any movement would be simple: probably both the killing and the capturing of the Piegans.
>
> I think the military commander [Colonel Baker] should be allowed to proceed generally according to circumstances under which he finds himself in his operations, having in view securing the fulfillment of our promises, etc., and the best interests of the frontier.

On January 15, 1870, General Sheridan responded by wire: "If the lives and property of the citizens of Montana can best be pro-tected by striking Mountain Chief's band of Piegans, I want them struck. Tell Baker to strike them hard!"

As procedure dictated, General de Trobriand then ordered the military action, under Baker's direction.

> You will proceed with your command . . . to chastise that portion of

the Indian tribe of Piegans which, under Mountain Chief or his sons, committed the greater part of the murders and depredations of last summer and last month in this district.

The band of Mountain Chief is now encamped on the Marias River, at a place called the Big Bend, and can be easily singled out from other bands of Piegans, two of which should be left unmolested, as they have uniformly remained friendly, viz., the bands of Heavy Runner and Big Lake. . . .

All necessary information in regard to the location of the several encampments and the character of the roaming Indians who may fall into your hands during your operations will be furnished you by the guide [Joe Kipp], who is ordered to report to you.

Beyond these general instructions, it is deemed unnecessary to add anything. The details as to the best way to surprise the enemy and to carry on the operations successfully are confidently left to your judgment and discretion, according to circumstances and to your experience in such expeditions.

The scene was set.

Colonel Baker's force did not leave Fort Shaw until the morning of January 19, 1870, delayed by howling winds, blinding snow, and temperatures that dipped to forty degrees below zero. Finally the column struck out: more than two hundred mounted men from the Second U.S. Cavalry, fifty-five mounted infantrymen plus seventy-five foot soldiers from the Thirteenth U.S. Infantry, and a civilian supply train, under the supervision of Paul McCormick. The detachment also included two scouts, Joe Kipp and Joe Cobell—the latter a Wolf Creek rancher who had married the younger sister of Mountain Chief. Finally, Horace and Nathan Clarke, bent on avenging their father's murder, accompanied the force.

Despite harsh winter conditions, the men covered twenty miles the first day, to a camp below Priest's Butte (near present-day Choteau). Here the column laid over until the following evening, since Baker had decided to travel only at night to prevent discovery. By the morning of January 21, the contingent made camp twenty-two miles to the northeast, at the mouth of Muddy Creek. The weather remained unrelentingly cold and windy.

During the next night, the column covered twenty miles and camped where a long arm of Pondera Coulee terminates at the dry fork of the Marias River. Through the day of January 22, the men shivered in a fireless camp, to minimize detection. When darkness fell, the party again pushed north through the snow, to intersect the Marias River. After covering about eleven miles, the soldiers surrounded and surprised the small camp of Gray Wolf, a friendly Pikuni. Under the threat imposed by a force of three hundred soldiers, the members of Gray Wolf's band revealed that the camps of Big Horn, Red Horn, and Mountain Chief were downstream.

Baker detailed a sergeant and ten enlisted men to ride twenty miles upstream to protect Reiplinger's fur post, and ordered McCormick's wagon train and the foot soldiers to guard Gray Wolf's village. Then, through the crisp darkness, his column moved as quickly as possible over the broken terrain, eight miles downstream to "the Big Bend of the Marias."

In the dark, Kipp and Cobell counted twenty-six Pikuni lodges on the river flat, and another eleven tents across the stream, on the north side. A herd of several hundred horses scattered through the trees downstream. Baker deployed his troops along the bluffs above the camp. More than two hundred marksmen trained .50-caliber rifles and carbines on the village.

Then, just as the southeastern sky began to dilute the darkness, Joe Kipp rushed to Baker. He broke his order of silence, shouting that he recognized the camp as that of Heavy Runner—the friendly chief who deserved protection. An enraged Baker ordered Kipp placed under guard, and shot if he made another sound.

But it was too late. Kipp's yelling had stirred the camp. Suddenly a man burst from one of the tepees and ran toward the soldiers on the bluffs, waving a paper and shouting. A single shot rang out, and Heavy Runner toppled dead in the snow. He still clutched the document given to him on January 1 by General Sully, attesting to his peaceful conduct and guaranteeing his safety.

The soldiers immediately opened fire, sending volley upon volley ripping through the skin tents. Confusion reigned as some of the Pikuni scattered into the brush to escape the barrage. A few reached the horse herd and galloped downstream, but the riflemen cut down the rest in a hail of shots.

The soldiers continued to fire into the village for almost one hour—long after anyone detected movement. Some of the marksmen shot at the bindings of the lodges, and the skin coverings fell onto their occupants, catching fire from the cooking fires and suffocating their inhabitants. The screams of children and the wails of men and women rose from the devastated camp.

Finally Baker ordered a cease-fire, and the cavalry mounted and charged down the bluffs into the demolished camp. With sabers drawn, they attacked the tepees, slashing and stabbing anyone who moved. As Private Walter McKay entered one of the last standing lodges, a young boy peeked from beneath a pile of buffalo robes and shot him pointblank. McKay fell dead—the only casualty to Baker's force during the entire campaign.

Baker's men secured the Pikuni horse herd and captured some survivors, whom they flushed from the brush or pulled from beneath the smoldering tepees. Through Kipp and Cobell, the colonel learned that Mountain Chief's camp was located farther downstream. So he ordered a detail to guard the horses and the prisoners, and to pile and torch the natives' supplies and possessions. With two hundred mounted men, in the morning light, he pushed downriver almost ten miles, to the mouth of present-day Dead Indian Coulee.

Here he discovered a village of seven lodges, hastily abandoned. Obviously Mountain Chief had been warned by a member of Heavy Runner's camp who had escaped during the initial confusion. Baker's men burned the tepees and their contents and, as night fell, encamped.

On January 24 Baker's column returned to "the Big Bend," where Kipp informed him that some of the Pikuni survivors carried smallpox. Because of the disease, the Colonel freed the 140 prisoners—leaving them to fend for themselves in the snow and cold. Since his men had torched their supplies, Baker left several cases of bacon and hardtack to feed the natives, until they could reach other Pikuni camps along the river. The colonel ordered the confiscation of the village's three hundred horses.

Baker had finished his work. His column rode upstream through the frigid weather, reaching Reiplinger's post on January 26 and returning to Fort Shaw on January 29. General de Trobriand immediately wired to General Sheridan:

> The expedition was a complete success. Colonel Baker just returned, having killed 173 Piegans, destroying 44 lodges, with all their winter supplies, robes, etc., and capturing over 300 horses. . . . Most of the murderers and marauders of last summer are killed, although [Owl Child] and Mountain Chief escaped with a few followers. . . . Report by mail will follow without delay.

By Baker's official count, 120 of the Pikuni killed were able-bodied men, and the remainder were women and children. He noted that 140 prisoners had been captured and then released. General de Trobriand effusively congratulated Baker and recommended him for a brevet. By February 5, Baker and his troops had returned to Fort Ellis. They had ridden more than six hundred miles in less than a month, and in Montana's most severe winter weather.

The *Helena Weekly Herald* with delight reported the violence on the Marias. Its account reflects the public response of the Territory's white settlers to this incident in the clash of cultures.

The deed is done. The murder of Malcolm Clarke has been avenged.

[47]

The guilty Indians have been punished, and a terrible warning has been given to others of our red-skinned brethren who may be inclined to live by murdering and plundering the white man.

The Pikuni accounts of this massacre on the Marias differ from the official government story. Bear Head, a survivor of the Baker attack, told his story to writer James Willard Schultz, author of *Blackfeet and Buffalo*. He explained that Heavy Runner's band had been joined by the bands of Red Horn and Big Horn to provide more bison meat for the families afflicted with smallpox. About one week before the attack, this group had moved into Mountain Chief's abandoned campsite at "the Big Bend of the Marias," because the area afforded better feed for their horse herd.

Bear Head maintained that most of the Pikuni men were not in the camp, but downriver, hunting bison. Thus the Pikuni count of the casualties read "15 men, 90 women, and 50 children; 44 lodges and lodge furnishings destroyed; hundreds of our horses stolen."

The figures cited by Bear Head approximate the casualties listed by the Blackfeet agent, Lieutenant William B. Pease. In a February 6, 1870, communiqué to his civilian-office superior, General Sully, Pease recounted,

> Of the 173 killed on the 23rd [of January], 33 were men. Of them, 15 only were such as are called by them young or fighting men—that is, men between the ages of 12 and 37 years. Ten were from 37 to 60 years, and 8 additional men were over 60 years. All in all, 33 men.
>
> There were 90 women killed: 55 (or over one-half) of whom were over 40 years of age; the remaining 35 women were between 12 and 40 years of age. Lastly there were 50 children under the age of 12 years killed. Many of them were in their mothers' arms.
>
> The whole village had been suffering for over two months past with smallpox, some half-dozen dying daily. Thus the village was relatively defenseless.

When General Sully forwarded this information to the Office of Indian Affairs in Washington, D.C., Vincent Colyer, secretary to the Board of Indian Commissioners, presented the figures to the U.S. House of Representatives. An emotional discussion ensued, pitting what General Sheridan termed "the Eastern Indian lovers" against the defenders of the military.

During this exchange, the nonvoting delegate to Congress from Montana Territory, James M. Cavanaugh, staunchly reflected his constituents' position. When asked, by Representative George F. Hoar of Massachusetts, if he approved "the killing of these women and children in cold blood, when there were no weapons in their hands," Cavanaugh responded:

I will answer the question . . . in the words of General [William S.] Harney, after the Battle of Ash Hollow [on the Platte River in 1855]. When he was assailed for killing squaws and papooses at Ash Hollow, he said, "They are nits and will become lice, and it is better to kill them in their chrysalis state." I endorse the act of Colonel Baker upon this occasion.

Nevertheless, national repercussions did develop from the massacre on the Marias. A proposal then before Congress would have transferred the Office of Indian Affairs from the Department of the Interior back to the War Department, from whence it had been moved in 1849. Because of the Montana incident, the proposal suffered a resounding defeat. Similarly, the standing policy of assigning military personnel as Indian agents became a legislative casualty of the Baker attack. In 1870 Congress forbade army officers to hold any civilian appointments.

Colonel Baker failed to submit a report covering his campaign until two months after the incident. The account he finally filed proved remarkably brief and lacking in detail. Yet in Montana, Baker's actions produced loud applause. Montanans continued to argue the righteousness of his actions. Ten years after the military victory, U.S. Marshal William F. Wheeler noted,

> The results of Baker's campaign are not underrated by the people of Montana, and they cannot be appreciated by Eastern people, because they do not know the danger which was averted in our case, and they have forgotten their own Indian wars.
>
> Ever since January, 1870, the Blackfeet tribes . . . have been peaceable and quiet, and it has been safe to travel all over their country. Very few white men have since been murdered by them, and [those who have] were generally whiskey traders and characters dangerous in any community, and they caused their own calamities. The punishment of the Piegans has had a most salutary effect on the conduct of all the other tribes in Montana.

Inexplicably, the federal government conducted no official inquiry into the massacre on the Marias. Colonel Baker did not receive a reprimand, a demotion—or a promotion. He acquired, however, a sort of immortality, by having his name linked with this notorious conflict.

On a bitingly cold January morning, at an isolated spot near "the Big Bend of the Marias," Baker proved that, when two cultures clash, the outcome can be ugly and searingly painful.

CHAPTER 4

LOST IN YELLOWSTONE:
THE AGONY OF TRUMAN EVERTS

Montanans who frequent their state's backcountry face the specter of being lost in the wilds. The realization that you have become disoriented and that you are isolated usually is followed by disbelief, anger, and then panic. When this fear recedes a bit, you are left to assess your priorities and to ponder how to escape the predicament. Often the question of whether your escape proves successful—whether you will be found—depends upon your ability to make wise decisions and practice the skills of survival. Being lost in the Montana wilds frequently becomes a matter of life and death.

Montana history abounds with accounts of individuals and small parties lost in rugged mountains, plains blizzards, remote river canyons, and broken prairie terrain. The scene replays several times a month, particularly during hunting seasons. The development of local search-and-rescue units offers but one response to the problem. In a state of few people and vast lands (even now there exist more than a hundred acres of land for each resident), the prospect of becoming lost in the wilderness remains very real for outdoors enthusiasts.

The thought of vanishing into the landscape never crossed the mind of Truman Everts in August 1870, as he prepared for an expedition to explore the mysterious wonders of the upper Yellowstone country. Everts, then fifty-four years old, had been born in Burlington,

Vermont, one of six sons of a ship's captain. In his youth, Truman received a public-school education and served his father as a cabin boy on several voyages on the Great Lakes.

Everts married a New England girl, and she bore him a daughter, Bessie, in 1852. Bessie became the focus of Truman's life after the untimely death of his wife. With the help of politically active friends, Everts received an appointment as the assessor of Internal Revenue for the fledgling Territory of Montana from President Abraham Lincoln in 1864. Soon he and Bessie moved to Virginia City, then the Territorial capital.

In 1869, however, Everts became the victim of the patronage intrigues of the Ulysses S. Grant administration, and he lost that federal position. He and Bessie then removed to Helena, in hope of obtaining suitable employment there. He could find no other job in Montana that he wanted, so Truman sent Bessie east in May 1870, and sold his furnishings at auction in June. He planned to return to "the States" himself early in the fall.

In July 1870, some Helena friends invited him to join an exploring escapade in the relatively unknown upper Yellowstone River country. He thought such an outing would serve as a fitting conclusion to his stay in the West. Thus Truman C. Everts became a member of the Washburn–Doane Expedition to that area which two years later would become Yellowstone National Park, the nation's first national park.

For decades tales of the wonders of the Yellowstone Lake region had been told by Native Americans, mountain men, and prospectors. These descriptions seemed so fantastic that few persons believed them. With the rush of "civilization" to Montana, as a result of placer-gold discoveries in the 1860s, the Yellowstone stories became even more intriguing. If just a shred of truth existed in the tales of boiling rivers, remarkable geysers, weird rock formations, tremendous cascades, and abundant big game, then commercial potential might exist for what was known as "Colter's Hell," after mountain man John Colter.

LOST IN YELLOWSTONE
AUGUST-OCTOBER, 1870

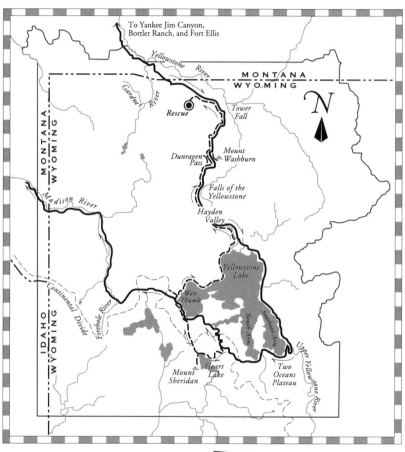

To Yankee Jim Canyon,
Bottler Ranch, and Fort Ellis

Yellowstone River

MONTANA
WYOMING

Gardner River

Rescue

Tower
Fall

N

MONTANA
WYOMING

Dunraven
Pass

Mount
Washburn

Madison River

Falls of the
Yellowstone

Hayden
Valley

Yellowstone
Lake

IDAHO
WYOMING

Continental Divide

Firehole River

West
Thumb

South Arm

Southeast Arm

Upper Yellowstone River

Mount
Sheridan

Heart
Lake

Two
Oceans
Plateau

Route of the Expedition ——
Everts's Route ----

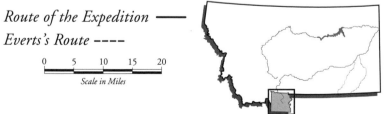

0	5	10	15	20

Scale in Miles

In the summer of 1869, three Diamond City men—David E. Folsom, C. W. Cook, and William Peterson—had engaged in the first trip by whites to the Yellowstone headwaters designed solely to determine the area's character. Because they wished to keep their reputations as honest men, however, they remained tight-lipped about the marvels they had encountered. Afterward, Folsom accepted a job in the Helena office of the surveyor general of Montana Territory, Henry D. Washburn. During the winter of 1869-1870, Folsom began to share stories of his trip, which inspired Washburn—a former general in the Union Army—to organize another visit to the "Wonderland."

These plans became reality with the arrival in Helena of Nathaniel P. Langford, the former federal collector of Internal Revenue for Montana Territory. Langford, who would become the first superintendent of Yellowstone National Park, anxiously wished to verify the tales of the Yellowstone Lake region. He prompted Washburn to request a military escort from Fort Ellis, near Bozeman, for the party. Thus, added to the original group from Helena, were Lieutenant Gustavus C. Doane and five other military men.

On August 17, 1870, the civilian participants in the Washburn-Doane Expedition trailed out on their journey's first leg, to Fort Ellis. In addition to Washburn, Langford, and Everts, the adventurers included:

—Warren C. Gillette, operator of the highly successful mercantile/transportation enterprise of King and Gillette, and subsequently a territorial legislator and a member of the state's 1889 Constitutional Convention;

—Samuel T. Hauser, president of the first National Bank of Helena and later governor of Montana Territory;

—Cornelius Hedges, a partner in the law firm of Lawrence and Hedges and a regular contributor to the *Helena Herald*; subsequently he became the U.S. attorney for Montana Territory, and the Superintendent of Public Instruction;

—Jacob W. Smith, cofounder of the Montana Hide and Fur

Company, who later became a millionaire broker in San Francisco;

—Benjamin F. Stickney, manager of the freighting firm of Plant, Stickney and Ellis, then a successful mercantilist and stockman in the Craig, Montana, area;

—Walter Trumbell, Everts's assistant assessor of Internal Revenue and later the assistant U.S. consul to Zanzibar.

In addition, the party hired two packers, Elwyn Bean and Charley Reynolds, and two African American cooks, "Nute" and "Johnny."

By the time the group reached Fort Ellis, Lieutenant Doane had received his orders to accompany the expedition and protect it against possible encounters with hostile Indian bands reportedly in the upper Yellowstone area. Doane's detail included Sergeant William A. Baker and Privates Charles Moore, John Williamson, George W. McConnell, and William Leipler. The expedition, which departed Fort Ellis on August 22, comprised nineteen men, about forty head of stock, provisions for thirty days, and a large "pavilion" tent, the contribution of Lieutenant Doane.

Spirits ran high as the party crossed into the Yellowstone Valley and reached the Bottler Ranch, opposite Emigrant Gulch. Everts—who, at fifty-four was ten years the senior of any other expedition member—had gorged himself on trailside berries and spent an uncomfortable night with the Bottler brothers.

By August 24 he had recovered, however, and the party pushed farther up the Yellowstone—through Yankee Jim Canyon, past Devil's Slide and the mouth of the Gardner River—reaching Tower Falls on August 27. The expedition then skirted what would later be called Mount Washburn, climbed through Dunraven Pass, and rejoined the river at the two falls of the Yellowstone. As the number of natural wonders daily increased, so did the enthusiasm of the company.

Under the direction of Doane and Washburn, the men rode south through the Hayden Valley, crossing the Yellowstone River at Nez Perce Ford and striking the shore of Yellowstone Lake on September 3. Following an impromptu operation on Lieutenant Doane's infected thumb—performed by Nathaniel Langford with a dull penknife—the mounted group threaded its way around the east side of the lake. Masses of fallen timber and marshy bogs impeded their progress. By September 7, the explorers had crossed the Upper Yellowstone River and rounded the Southeast Arm of Yellowstone Lake.

September 8 proved the most difficult travel day yet faced by the expedition. Impenetrable slopes of closely knit "doghair" pine and downed timber covered the south end of the lake. The men necessarily spread out, picked individual routes, and helped their saddle horses and pack animals through this labyrinth. During the day they traveled only four miles and had not reached South Arm when most of the explorers quit fighting the obstacles and made camp for the night.

That evening Cornelius Hedges and Truman Everts climbed a north promontory of the Two Ocean Plateau to survey their situation. Although Everts was very nearsighted, he scanned the terrain with the aid of his spectacles and a small pair of opera glasses. The two men selected what they believed would be an easier route for the next day and returned to camp after dark—just as the last few members of the party straggled in from a long, frustrating day of fighting the forest maze.

September 9 proved little different, however. Members of the group again separated so they could pick individual routes through the "doghair" and downed timber. Sometime that afternoon, west of South Arm, Truman Everts found himself alone in the forest tangle and realized that he had disengaged completely from his companions.

Shortly he encountered one of the expedition's unattended pack horses and attempted to drive him through the forest. This only led him farther from the course he thought his companions had chosen. He then abandoned the pack horse and tried to locate the group's camp on his own. Because of the alignment of the Continental Divide in the area, however, he confused directions. Instead of heading northwest toward the Flat Mountain Arm of Yellowstone Lake, he actually wandered southwest, into the Snake River drainage. When dark fell on the forest maze, Everts picketed his saddle horse, built a campfire, and prepared to spend the night. He had never passed a night alone in the woods before, but that prospect did not overly concern him.

As the other explorers struggled into camp that evening, they gradually realized that Everts was missing. They fired signal shots, and two men retraced the general route to search, unsuccessfully. Still, no one became seriously worried. Everts had demonstrated some rudimentary skill at woodsmanship on the trip, and he *had* viewed the entire terrain the preceding evening from the Two Ocean Plateau. They concluded that he either would rejoin the party the next day, or would meet them at the prearranged campsite on the lakeshore at West Thumb.

On September 10, Everts broke camp at daybreak, but met with difficulty in the dense forest. He found no sign of his mates. Because of his poor vision, he dismounted frequently to examine the forest floor for tracks—and during one such instance disaster struck. Everts, in the romanticized account of his experiences that later appeared in *Scribner's Magazine*, described this misfortune:

> In searching for the trail, I became somewhat confused. . . . Coming to an opening, from which I could see several vistas, I dismounted for the purpose of selecting one [trail] leading in the direction I had chosen. Leaving my horse unhitched, as had always been my custom, I walked a few rods into the forest.
>
> While surveying the ground, my horse took flight, and I turned around in time to see him disappearing at full speed among the trees. That was the last I ever saw of him. My blankets, gun, pistols, fishing tackle, matches—everything except the clothing on my person, a couple of knives, and a small opera-glass—were attached to the saddle.

Truman spent half that day trying to follow and recover his horse. After wandering through the woods in this unsuccessful attempt, he became truly disoriented and hopelessly lost. He wrote and posted a number of messages on tree trunks in clearings northeast of Heart Lake. He then settled down for a night in the wilderness without either food or fire, in temperatures dropping below freezing. Reality set in:

> Naturally timid in the night, I fully realized the exposure of my condition. I peered upward through the darkness, but all was blackness and gloom. The wind sighed mournfully through the pines. The forest seemed alive with the screeching of night birds, the angry barking of coyotes, and the prolonged, dismal howl of the gray wolf.
>
> My disappointment was almost overwhelming. For the first time I realized that I was lost. Then came a crushing sense of destitution. No food, no fire, and no means to procure either. Alone in an unexplored wilderness, 150 miles from the nearest human abode, surrounded by wild beasts, and famishing with hunger. . . . But it was not time for despondency.

On September 11, near midday, Everts broke out of the forest on the northeast shore of Heart Lake. His wanderings had kept him on the western slope of the Continental Divide, and he remained in the Snake River drainage.

On the same day, the expedition reached the prearranged site on the south shore of Yellowstone Lake's West Thumb. During the preceding night the men had set a large signal fire on a ridge above the lake, but Everts never saw it. Nor, from his dense-forest location, did he hear another round of signal shots fired on the other side of the Divide. Since no sign at the West Thumb site indicated that Everts had preceded them, the explorers made camp and planned a thorough search.

Everts fortunately discovered a food source at Heart Lake: the radish-like root of a thistle, abundant in the area. However, if he needed a reaffirmation of his vulnerability, he received it on the first night spent on the lakeshore. He had laid a bed of boughs under a tree and fallen asleep, when:

> Suddenly I was aroused by a loud, shrill scream—like that of a human being in distress—seemingly poured into the portals of my ears. There was no mistaking that fearful voice. I had been deceived by it, and answered it, a dozen times while threading through the forest, with the belief that it was a friendly signal. It was, in truth, the screech of a mountain lion, so alarmingly near as to cause my every nerve to thrill with terror.

Everts quickly climbed the tree and traded screams with the lion as it stalked in circles beneath him. He tried hurling broken branches at the beast, which he could only hear, and not see, in the darkness. Finally he resorted to silence, and this tactic proved effective. The cat prowled off into the woods, never taking the jump into the tree that would have forced Everts into combat. This outcome was particularly lucky, since he had lost both of his knives in the climb—and he never would recover them.

Everts returned to his bed at the base of the tree, but in several hours an autumn storm of rain, sleet, and snow, propelled by a strong easterly wind, awakened him. This storm series would continue for five days. With a large supply of fibrous thistle roots, he spent nearly two days huddled in a shallow cavern formed by an uprooted tree. He had no fire, and his torn clothing provided little protection from the storm, but at least his fast had ended.

During the second day of the storm, Everts abandoned his cavern, worked his way around the north side of Heart Lake through the new snow, waded its inlet, and entered the geyser basin at the foot of Mount Sheridan. Here he sought shelter and warmth for his now-frostbitten feet.

> I selected a spot between two springs sufficiently asunder to afford

heat at my head and feet. On this spot I built a bower of pine branches. Thistles were abundant, and I cooked them from time to time in a boiling spring nearby.

This shelter I occupied for seven days [September 13-19, 1870], the first three of which were darkened by one of the most furious storms I ever saw. The vapor which supplied me with warmth saturated my torn clothing with its condensations. I was enveloped in a perpetual steam-bath. At first this was barely preferable to the storm, but I soon became accustomed to it and, before I left, I actually enjoyed it—though thoroughly parboiled.

Everts's privations began to extract a toll. His lack of food and his gathering panic produced miscalculations and disappointments. While on the shore of Heart Lake, he once believed rescue imminent.

The fear of meeting with Indians gave me considerable anxiety. But, when conscious of being lost, there was nothing I so much desired as to fall in with a lodge of Bannocks or Crows. Having nothing to tempt their cupidity, I was sure they would do me no personal harm. And, with the promise of reward, they would probably minister to my wants and aid my deliverance.

Imagine my delight, while gazing upon the animated expanse of water, at seeing sail out from a distant point a large canoe containing a single oarsman. It was rapidly approaching the shore where I was seated. With hurried steps I paced the beach to meet it, all my energies stimulated by the assurance it gave of food, safety, and restoration of friends.

As I drew near, it turned towards the shore, and oh! bitter disappointment: the object which my eager fancy had transformed into an angel of relief stalked from the water—an enormous pelican—flapped its dragon-wings as if in mockery of my sorrow, and flew to a solitary point farther up the lake.

This little incident quite unmanned me. The transition from joy to grief brought with it a terrible consciousness of the horrors of my condition.

In truth, while at Heart Lake, Everts nearly *was* rescued. From their West Thumb campsite, members of the expedition paired off to search back to the east and south. Unfortunately, the five-day storm soon obliterated any trace of Everts's trail under almost two feet of snow. However, his companions believed that Truman remained on horseback, so finding him should be just a matter of locating the valley in which he had camped and bringing him back.

Henry Washburn and Nathaniel Langford rode south from Yellowstone Lake, toward Mount Sheridan. When they reached a point less than one mile from Heart Lake, Langford's horse broke through a thin ground crust and scalded all four of its legs so severely in hot mud that the men decided to return to camp. From the site of the accident, the two searchers looked into the geyser basin—but they could not see Everts's shelter, obscured by the rising steam.

After searching for seven days, the explorers had found no trace of their companion. They concluded that he probably ran afoul of a band of outlaws, rumored to frequent the upper Snake River watershed. The group's leaders decided that the main party should continue west, cross into the Firehole Valley, and return to civilization by trailing down the Madison River. Yet even then they did not abandon Everts completely: Warren Gillette, one of the best woodsmen in the group, and Privates Williamson and Moore remained, with ten days' rations, to begin one final search.

During Everts's week-long stay at the Heart Lake hot springs, two events occurred that affected his chances of survival. First, one night, in a fitful sleep, he broke through a crustation and escaping steam grievously scalded his right thigh. This wound—combined with his frostbitten feet, just beginning to fester—rendered any travel both slow and painful. Second, while lying in his shelter, Everts pondered the problem of fire, since fire would be essential should he attempt to hike out, in freezing temperatures, through the snow. Everts recalled his situation:

> At a break in the storm, a gleam of sunshine lit up the bosom of the lake, and with it the thought flashed upon my mind that I could, with the lens from my opera-glasses, get fire from Heaven. Oh, happy, life-renewing thought! I instantly subjected [my idea] to the test of experiment.
>
> When I saw the smoke curl from the bit of dry wood in my fingers, I felt that, if the whole world were offered me for that little spark, I would cast it all aside before parting with it. I was now the happy possessor of food and fire.

Encouraged by his discovery of fire and by a revised sense of direction, Truman departed Heart Lake on September 19. He planned to push north, recross the Continental Divide, and drop down to the shore of Yellowstone Lake at West Thumb. This attempt, however, proved unsuccessful. At the end of an arduous day of hiking, the weakened adventurer found himself short of the Divide on an exposed hillside, without any sunlight to produce fire.

Everts spent a frigid night and returned to Heart Lake the next afternoon. He built a fire on the lakeshore and spent two days recovering. Repeatedly he damned his injuries, his waning strength, and his predicament—surrounded by birds, fish, and animals, he could find no way to kill them for food.

Not only had Everts failed to reach Yellowstone Lake on his attempt, but he also inadvertently had eluded the Gillette rescue party. These three men had ridden east from West Thumb to the downed-timber area where Everts had disappeared on September 9. They then worked their way down to Heart Lake, reaching it on the morning of September 20. From its outlet they scanned the shoreline and the geyser basin for campfire smoke and a saddle horse. Seeing neither, they continued down the Heart River to its confluence with the Snake.

The squad finally exited the area via the Madison Valley, following the trail of the expedition.

Had the three men searched the geyser basin at Heart Lake, they would have found Everts's bower. Had they arrived at the lake several hours later, they would have seen the smoke from his lakeshore fire. Unknown to Everts, he *really* would be alone from this point.

On September 23, Everts again left Heart Lake to try to cross the Divide and reach West Thumb. He had been separated from his party for fifteen days by this time. His diet consisted solely of thistle roots, and he was losing weight and stamina rapidly. His eyesight was limited, as was his wilderness experience; his feet had become painfully infected; his scalded thigh was excruciatingly raw. And he already knew how quickly winter storms could descend on this high country—ranging above eight thousand feet—and hinder any travel.

Everts's opera glasses could provide fire if the sun shone, and he had cut a pair of leather sandals from his dilapidated boots, with a crude knife fashioned from his belt buckle. Otherwise he stood defenseless against the elements, wild animals, and attacks on his sanity. A betting man would not have accepted odds on his chances of survival in "Wonderland."

Nevertheless, by September 25, Everts had hobbled the ten miles over the Divide to the expedition's campsite on West Thumb. He forestalled the lack of sunny weather by carrying a firebrand the entire way. On the shore of Yellowstone Lake, he found the old campsite, abandoned, and the effect proved debilitating: "Oh! Why did they forget to leave food? I left the camp in deep dejection."

Before leaving, however, Everts scavenged the area. He recovered a fork, which became a root-digging tool, and a small baking-powder can, which became a drinking cup and cooking pot.

From West Thumb, Everts's initial attempt followed the westward route of the departed expedition over to the Firehole Valley, then downstream along the Madison River. However, he encountered difficulty finding his companions' trail. Again disoriented, he finally kindled a campfire from his firebrand and made night camp in a howling wind, on a forested mountainside.

> How long I slept I know not, but I was aroused by the snapping and crackling of the burning foliage, to find my shelter and the adjacent forest in a broad sheet of flame. My left hand was badly burned and my hair was singed, closer than a barber would have trimmed it, while making my escape from the semicircle of burning trees. Among the disasters of this fire, there was none I felt more seriously than the loss of my belt-buckle knife.

Everts had set the entire mountainside afire, but even this conflagration signaled no rescuers—all of whom, except the Gillette party, had returned to Fort Ellis and Helena by this time.

Discouraged by the formidable westward route, Truman dragged himself back to the shore of Yellowstone Lake. He determined to follow its shoreline north and then work downstream, along the Yellowstone River, until he intersected the trail that the expedition had used to enter the Yellowstone region. This route stretched much farther, but it offered an easier terrain, and some of the track would be familiar to him.

So, on September 29, he started his slow, painful trek to the north. Quickly he found that loss of physical stamina was not his only problem. His mental stability became equally crucial, and it too had begun to diminish. When Everts questioned his own decision to follow the northward route, he received advice from an unexpected source:

> I experienced one of those strange hallucinations which many of my friends have misnamed insanity, but which to me was Providence. An old clerical friend, for whose character and counsel I had always cherished particular regard, in some unaccountable manner seemed to be standing before me, charged with advice which would relieve my perplexity.

"Travel [to the north] as fast and as far as possible," he said. "It is your only chance."

"Doctor," I replied, "I am rejoined to meet you in this hour of distress, but doubt the wisdom of your counsel. . . my shoes are nearly worn out, my clothes are in tatters, and my strength is almost overcome."

"Don't think of it," he rejoined. "Your powers of endurance will carry you through. I will accompany you. Put your trust in Heaven. Help yourself and God will help you."

Overcome by these and other persuasions—and delighted with the idea of having a traveling companion—I plodded my way over the route. . . . Whenever I was disposed, as was often the case, to question the wisdom of this route, my old friend appeared with words of encouragement.

As Everts bumbled along the lakeshore and pushed into the Hayden Valley, he also drew courage from a catch phrase that had played through his mind from the very first day of his separation from his companions: "I *will not* perish in this wilderness!" The line became litany, chanted as he battled the obstacles of his march. From it he drew both hope and strength.

His daughter Bessie served as his other source of inspiration:

As I struggled along, my thought would revert to the single being on whom my holiest affections centered—my daughter. What a tie was that to bind me to life! Oh! Could I be restored to her for a single hour, long enough for parting counsel and blessing, it would be joy unspeakable! Long hours of painful travel were relieved of physical suffering by this absorbing agony of the mind.

At this point, Truman Everts had been lost for almost four weeks. His weight had dropped below eighty pounds, his tattered clothing provided no protection from the elements, and both sleep and food had lost importance to him. His companions had all but abandoned hope of ever seeing him alive.

Sparks from the lighted brands had burned my hands and crisped the nails of my fingers, and the smoke from them had tanned my face to the complexion of an Indian.

I lost all sense of time. Days and nights came and went, and were numbered only by the growing consciousness that I was gradually starving. I felt no hunger; I did not eat to appease appetite, but to renew strength.

I experienced but little pain. The gaping sores on my feet, the severe burn on my hip, the festering crevices at the joints of my fingers—all terrible in appearance—had ceased to give me the least concern. The roots which supplied my food had suspended the digestive power of the stomach, and their fibers were packed in it in a matted, compact mass.

In dreams that accompanied fitful periods of sleep, Everts traveled to the most exquisite restaurants in New York City, Baltimore, and Washington, D.C. There he enjoyed sumptuous dinners of the most elegantly prepared delicacies. At one point the organs of his body—particularly his stomach, his arms, and his legs—assumed personae. He thereafter carried on discussions with this group of fellow travelers. Reality became progressively elusive. This condition was only accentuated when he broke his spectacles, rendering himself virtually sightless.

Slowly crawling along the expedition's incoming route, Everts passed the Upper and Lower Falls of the Yellowstone, recrossed Dunraven Pass, and reached Tower Falls. He had developed an intense, desperate hatred for such spectacular natural wonders:

They had lost all charm for me. In fact, I regarded them as enemies which had lured me to destruction. I felt a sullen satisfaction in my morbid indifference to them. . . . The grand and massive scenery which, on the upward journey, had aroused every enthusiastic impulse of my nature, was now tame and spiritless.

Early in October, another snowstorm confused Everts; it forced him to return to the river to regain his bearings. He sought refuge from the storm in the Yellowstone River canyon—dropping down then climbing back up its rugged walls.

Shortly after this storm broke, and he had resumed his trek, Everts dropped the opera glasses and had to retrace his path for about five miles to recover his only source of heat, light, and protection. Then another storm of several days' duration hit. Rather than hole up in his extremely weakened condition, Everts followed the advice of his body and continued dragging himself northward along the trail.

On October 9—still trapped in the intermittent snow and sleet squalls, with his firebrand extinguished—Everts's ordeal ended at a place called "The Cut":

Groping along the side of a hill, I became suddenly sensible of a sharp reflection, as of burnished steel. Looking up, through half-closed eyes, two rough but kindly faces met my gaze.

"Are you Mr. Everts?" one of them said.

After being lost alone in "Wonderland" for thirty-seven days, struggling sixty halting, serpentine miles, and losing almost one hundred pounds, a gaunt Truman Everts was rescued by two mountain men, John "Yellowstone Jack" Baronett and George A. Pritchett. The men had been searching for Everts because of a $600 reward posted for his recovery by Cornelius Hedges's law partner, Judge Robert Lawrence of Helena.

Baronett, who would become one of the legendary characters of Yellowstone National Park history, recalled the discovery distinctly:

There was an icy sleet falling. There had been two feet of snow on the ground earlier, but it had disappeared. This sleet was barely making the ground white, but I noticed that my dog had found some kind of trail. By looking closely, I saw that something had dragged itself along upon the ground. I decided that some hunter had wounded a bear and that it was trying to make its way up to the mountains, and out of curiosity I followed on.

When I had trailed the wounded bear for a mile or more, my dog began to growl and, looking across a small canyon to the mountainside beyond, I saw a black object upon the ground. Yes, sure enough, there was my Bruin. My first impulse was to shoot him from where I stood, but as he was going so slowly I saw that I should have no difficulty in overtaking him, and I crossed over to where he was.

When I got near to it, I found it was not a bear, and for my life I could not tell what it was. It did not look like any animal that I had ever seen, and it was certainly not a human being. It never occurred to me that it was Everts. I went up close to the object; it was making a low, groaning noise, crawling upon its knees and elbows, and trying to drag itself up the mountain. Then it suddenly occurred to me that it was the object of my search. I spoke his name. . . .

Poor fellow, he was nothing but a shadow! His flesh was all gone. The bones protruded through the skin on the balls of his feet and thighs. His fingers looked like bird's claws. I carried him down to [a creek], built a fire, made some tea, and gave him a spoonful.

Baronett and Pritchett began nursing Everts back to health. They moved him first to a campsite several miles down the trail. The next day, Baronett carried him on his horse another eleven miles downstream to a miners' cabin on Turkey Pen Creek. Pritchett then departed for Fort Ellis to announce the rescue and to return with a wagon and a doctor, while Baronett coaxed mild foods into the emaciated victim.

Everts's digestive system, clogged with thistle-root fiber, continued to cause him excruciating pain. However, a mountain man who stopped by the cabin solved that problem. He rendered a pint of bear grease from a recent kill and had Everts drink the hot oil. By the next day, the remedy had delivered Truman of his stomach pain, and he embarked on the path to recovery.

The wagon carrying Everts did not reach Fort Ellis until October 24. Two days later, friends moved him to Bozeman, where they cared for him for another two weeks. Finally, on November 4, 1870, Truman Everts returned to Helena—which he had left eighty days earlier. Almost one-half of those days he had been lost in the wilderness.

Everts's condition had improved remarkably by that time. He still walked with a slight limp, and his right arm retained some numbness. Yet his weight had climbed back up over a hundred pounds, and his spirits were high.

On November 12, the members of the Washburn-Doane Yellowstone Expedition held a banquet at the Kan Kan Restaurant in Helena to celebrate Everts's remarkable survival. Given Truman's starvation, the elaborate menu comprised the stuff of his most exotic dreams:

SOUP: Oyster
OYSTERS: Raw and roasted
FISH: Mountain trout
BOILED MEATS: Leg of mutton with capers; tongue with egg sauce; ham; chicken
ROAST MEATS: Beef; chicken; mutton; breast of lamb with green peas; breast of veal with white sauce
ENTREES: Spring chicken; breaded veal and mushrooms; sweet breads; oyster patties
VEGETABLES: Sweet potatoes; green corn; tomatoes; asparagus; string beans; cauliflower
RELISHES: Celery; horseradish; piccalilli pickles; beets
PASTRY-PIES: Green pear; peach; cranberry; gooseberry

PUDDINGS: Peach meringue; strawberry; custard
DESSERT: Fruit cake; pound cake; jelly cake; citron cake; jelly roll; jelly tarts; tart cream; strawberry cream; puff paste; raisins; confections
COFFEE: Mocha
WINES: Champagne; Imperial

Shortly after the banquet, Truman Everts traveled back to "the States," to reunite with his daughter and to work in minor federal positions in Washington, D.C. He reappeared in Bozeman late in the 1870s, as one of the post traders at Fort Ellis. He then returned to Hyattsville, Maryland, where he married for a second time at the age of sixty-five. At age seventy-five, Everts fathered a son. He lived another decade before dying in Hyattsville in 1901. Obviously he had recovered quite well from his harrowing experience in the Yellowstone country.

Historians widely praise the members of the Washburn-Doane Expedition as the first to verify and publicize the marvels of the upper Yellowstone Valley. Their trip played a major role in the movement to preserve that remarkable area. In 1872, when Congress created Yellowstone as the nation's first national park, authorities offered the position of superintendent to Truman Everts. He declined in favor of his friend Nathaniel Langford.

No historical evidence shows that Everts ever returned to the site of his thirty-seven days of peril. Little wonder. Lost once in that wilderness, it consumed every bit of his determination to escape its grasp.

CHAPTER 5

MONTANA'S WOLF WARS

*Only the mountain has lived long enough
to listen objectively to the howl of the wolf.*

——*Aldo Leopold,* A Sand County Almanac, *1949*

Aldo Leopold might have been speaking directly to Montanans when he reflected on man's relationship with the wolf. For this issue has remained hotly partisan and intensely volatile—beginning with the earliest confrontation between Montana stockmen and the wolf in the 1880s. Finally, during the Great Depression, a ranchers' decade-long campaign eliminated the wolf from the Montana landscape. Now, however, with the return of wolves to several areas of the state, the story of the wolf in Montana deserves a measured telling.

Before the European settlement of North America, commencing in earnest in the seventeenth century, the gray wolf (*Canis lupus*) inhabited lands from coast to coast and from northern Canada to central Mexico. In fact, this wolf enjoyed the widest distribution of any land mammal, a testament to his ability to adapt to diverse environments. One subspecies proved most prevalent across Montana: *Canis lupus nubilus.* Estimates of wolf population in Montana in 1800 run as high as 200,000 animals. Biologists currently figure the number at fewer than 100.

The adult Montana wolf stands 30 to 38 inches high, weighs between 80 and 125 pounds, and stretches from 5 to 6 feet long, including the tail. He can live more than thirteen years, although most do not reach five years of age. At a full run, a wolf can hit 40 miles per hour, but he maintains a more normal, slow trot of 5 miles per hour in open country for hours on end. As a result, a wolf can cover as much as 100 miles per day—though a more normal-day course, in search of food, covers 20 miles. A wolf's regular hunting foray often comprises a 60-mile circle.

The wolf is a carnivore, who kills to eat, so the availability of food dictates his hunting region. He accepts a lifetime mate, but if that companion dies, he will breed with another. Together the pair raises a series of litters, each of which can number six or eight pups or more.

The tendency of wolves to form a pack results from both the family's social organization and the size of its prey. For example, a pack of twenty wolves may form to stalk a bison or a moose, but that number is excessive when hunting ground squirrels. In hunting wild game, the wolf most often selects young, aged, or weak victims, because the kill is easier.

When the Lewis and Clark expedition crossed Montana in 1805 and 1806, its members encountered numerous wolves. They found them particularly on the plains, feeding on bison, but also in the wooded mountains. To these explorers, familiar with Eastern and Mid-western wolves, the Montana wolves proved more bothersome than remarkable. Journal entries addressing wolves lack the captains' usual descriptive detail.

A minor exception occurred for William Clark, moving down the lower Yellowstone River valley in early August 1806. He remarked:

> Saw emence numbers of Elk Buffalow and wolves to day. the wolves do catch the elk. I saw 2 wolves in pursute of a doe Elk which I beleive they Cought. they were very near her when She entered a Small wood in which I expect they cought her, as She did not pass out of the small wood during my remaining in view of it, which was 15 or 20 minits &c.

Hard on the heels of the Lewis and Clark expedition arrived the fur trappers, descending from the north and ascending the Missouri

MONTANA'S WAR
WITH THE WOLF
1880-1990

River from the southeast. Until 1840, however, the fur industry relied on the beaver trade. So mountain men ignored the wolf pelt, an
unprofitable commodity. In fact, trappers perceived the wolf primarily in the role of spoiler: the raider of animals from their trap sets
and the scavenger of food from their supply caches.

About 1850, however, the fur trade shifted its emphasis from beaver to buffalo hides, wolf pelts, and deer skins. As long as the bison
herds lasted (into the early 1880s), the buffalo hide dominated this
skin trade. Nevertheless mackinaws and steamboats consistently
freighted wolf pelts down the Missouri River to St. Louis. The American Fur Company shipped only twenty wolf pelts from Fort Benton
in 1850, but by 1853 that number had risen to more than three

thousand. During the mid-1860s, wolf pelts annually ran between five and ten thousand, collected from Company posts along the Missouri.

The abundance of wolves in Montana between 1860 and 1885 spawned an occupation peculiar to the Great Plains: the "wolfer." As long as a market remained for wolf pelts, men who worked seasonally on the steamboats, or in freighting or mining, resorted to "wolfing" during the winter, when the wolf pelt became prime. Such entrepreneurs needed a stake of only $150 to purchase a season's worth of staples and large supplies of ammunition and strychnine. With hard work, a man could gross as much as $2,000 by selling the wolf pelts at Fort Benton in the spring, for about $2.50 each.

The wolfer developed a relatively straightforward technique. He shot bison, at about five-mile intervals, in a circular pattern. He then implanted each carcass with strychnine, usually in crystalline-sulfate form, and proceeded down the line. Wolves trotted in to eat the fresh kill and were poisoned, dropping within yards of the carcass. On occasion, a single bait station could kill several dozen wolves. The wolfer continued to ride his circuit, skinning dead wolves and setting new poisoned carcasses. Observers have estimated that wolfers annually harvested more than 55,000 wolves between 1870 and 1877. The American Fur Company's cargo figures for its Missouri River posts during the 1870s reflect this estimate.

By the early 1880s, several outside forces changed the role played by the wolf on the Montana plains. First, wolfers had killed so many animals that wolfing became only marginally profitable, and many men abandoned the trade. Second, buffalo hunters rapidly were depleting the large bison herds on the plains. The last productive bison-hunting season in the Yellowstone Valley was 1881-1882; by 1884 only small groups of bison could be found scattered on the Montana prairies. As a result, the two parties most dependent on the bison—Native Americans and wolves—needed to adapt quickly to alternate food sources.

The third factor altering the wolf's role involved stockmen who, beginning in the 1870s, pushed small herds of domestic cattle from sheltered river valleys out onto public-domain prairies. These cattlemen had learned that range cattle could survive Montana winters by grazing on the nutritious native grasses. By the early 1880s, hundreds of cattle outfits were running massive herds on the plains that once had fed the bison.

The Montana plains wolf of the early 1880s faced no real choice in this situation. He could starve to death or change his diet from bison to cattle. This switch placed the wolf in direct conflict with Montana stockgrowers. For the next fifty years, the history of the Montana wolf comprises the story of the livestock industry's highly successful campaign to eliminate the wolf from the state.

The wolf long has preyed on domesticated cattle. The pattern developed in Europe even before it began in North America—wherever settlers brought cattle into the wolf's traditional habitat. Plymouth Colony placed the first American bounty on the wolf in 1630.

However, the open-range cattleman of the 1880s, using Montana's free grasses, faced an even greater threat from the wolf. For this stockman was not protecting a few milk cows around his log cabin, he was casting thousands of head across an unfenced landscape. He infrequently saw his cattle, and he held little control over their daily safety. This cattleman could sustain a substantial loss as a result of weather, theft, and predators. Yet, economically, he could not permit the large numbers of wolves roaming the Montana prairies to feast uncontested on his herds.

The open-range cattleman, working in a highly speculative industry, found in the wolf a convenient scapegoat for several of his problems. In addition the stockman cultivated a real hatred for the wolf, based on actions he believed demonstrated the animal's cowardice.

A wolf prefers a fresh kill, whenever available. He will begin eating a calf while it is still alive. He also will desert a carcass when sated, sometimes after consuming only twenty or thirty pounds of hind-quarters and entrails. Thus the rancher would find several dead calves on the range, each only partially eaten. He concluded that the wolf exemplified a wasteful predator, one that killed simply for the sport of it.

In the early 1880s, Montana stockmen initiated a fevered publicity campaign that anthropomorphized this *bete noire*. They invested the wolf with human characteristics—the worst human characteristics—not unlike the role assigned the animal in *Little Red Riding Hood*. An 1882 editorial by S. A. Marney in the (Miles City) *Stockgrowers Journal* illustrates this public-relations effort:

> In our territory alone, stock worth many thousands of dollars is annually devoured by wolves and other wild beasts. . . . The most feasible method of ridding the country of these destructive inhabitants seems to be the lavish, universal, and persistent use of poison. . . .
>
> Let every man who rides the range, or has men riding it, regard it as his special duty to spread as much destruction in the form of poison as possible. It will finally tell, and much money will be saved annually to the stockman.

Strychnine was not the open-range rancher's only weapon in the crusade. Some cattlemen purchased packs of greyhounds and similarly blooded dogs to run the wolves; others relied on traps, snares, lariats, and rifles to kill the predators. One of the most effective methods involved locating a wolf den in the spring. Cowhands would dig out the lair or dynamite it, killing the female and her newborn litter of pups. Some ranchers even hired cowboys who worked solely as "wolfers" on their range.

The "wolf problem"—as popularly known on the Montana plains in the early 1880s—proved one of several factors that convinced ranchers that livestock associations had become necessary to benefit the industry. Local stock groups and the Montana Stock Growers

Association lobbied the territorial legislature to create a bounty on range predators—the bear, the mountain lion, the coyote, and especially the wolf.

Passed by the 1883 assembly, the first Montana bounty law provided that the territorial government would pay $1 for each wolf hide presented to the probate judge or justice of the peace. The bounty hunter then could sell the skin privately, which usually brought another $1 to $2.50, depending on its condition. The stockmen believed that, at about $3 per wolf, it would become profitable for hunters to return to the occupation of wolfing. Their belief proved correct.

The Montana bounty law changed through the decades, revised as stockmen's pressure on the legislature waxed and waned. Following the "Hard Winter of 1886-1887," surviving Montana cowmen renewed their campaign to rid their range (now rapidly being fenced) of the wolf. The bounty provided $2 per pelt (1891), and the amount rose until it peaked at $15 (1911). In addition to the state bounty, some counties, cattlemen's associations, and sheep ranchers' groups provided high supplemental bounties. And hunters still could sell the pelt on the open market.

During the 1890s, wolf hunters often could clear fourteen dollars per kill, and that amount rendered the work profitable. The higher prices for wolves produced an increased number of kills. During a six-month period in 1895, the State of Montana paid a bounty on 2,978 wolves; in 1896 it paid for 5,866; in 1897, 4,995; in 1898, 4,780; and in 1899, 3,832.

After the turn of the century, the number of wolves presented annually for the bounty declined. The legislature finally repealed the general bounty law in 1933. Nevertheless the bounty system performed effectively for the stockmen. It provided a real incentive for wolf hunters to reduce the predator's numbers. More important, it functioned as a visible weapon in the stockmen's public-relations campaign against the wolf. Raisers of horses, cattle, and sheep admittedly exaggerated their predator losses to argue for higher bounties. They then flooded newspapers with anti-wolf publicity, and that publicity in turn only intensified the stockmen's hatred of the wolf.

Early in the twentieth century, two factors combined to reduce the wolf population in Montana. First, the 1901 Legislature increased the bounty on wolf pups to five dollars each—the same premium it paid on an adult wolf. As a result, hunters concentrated on locating wolf dens in the spring and killing the she-wolf and her entire litter. This approach proved devastating to the propagation of the species. Second, a handful of operators who specialized in the elimination of wolves dominated the business.

Faced with these developments, local wolf populations suffered severe losses. Ranchers could be heard saying that the wolf had been eradicated in their areas—for instance, the Bitterroot, Gallatin, and Madison Valleys. Plains livestock growers did not agree, however. Their voices rose to a crescendo, demanding the extirpation of the *bete noire*. Because of the stockmen's campaign, the wolf had assumed a role far in excess of reality.

Homesteaders who covered Montana's high plains and forests between 1906 and 1918 administered the decisive blow. By inhabiting 160-acre plots across the prairies and wooded foothills, settlers encroached on the wolves' remaining denning sites, either displacing pregnant females or killing them. Simultaneously, the responsibility for the elimination of the wolf shifted from local livestock associations, counties, and the state to the federal government.

In 1915 the U.S. Department of Agriculture's Biological Survey accepted responsibility for controlling predators on all federal lands. The survey used its $125,000 allocation to hire government hunters/trappers to work areas where mountain lions, coyotes, and wolves were preying on livestock. By the time the survey's hunters entered the Montana arena, the wolf's numbers had decreased considerably. These professionals systematically attacked what wolves remained.

By the 1920s, the vast majority of Montana wolves had been

eliminated. As a result, two interesting sociocultural phenomena evolved. The first involved documenting the killing of the "last wolf" in an area. The second entailed identifying specific "renegade" wolves, to which stockmen attached names like "Snowdrift" and "the White Wolf of the Judith."

In the case of the "last wolf" phenomenon, the Montana media showed little remorse in reporting the killing. Decades of anti-wolf publicity, emanating from the livestock industry, could not be denied. A "last wolf" account, appearing in the (Helena) *Montana Record-Herald* in 1922, is illustrative:

HUNTER'S BULLET CLOSES CAREER OF OLD, LAST WOLF
Livingston. A notorious lone wolf, said to have killed during his lifetime more than $10,000 worth of cattle on the range of Wallis Huidekoper, well-known Montana stockman and president of the state stockmen's association, is no more. The head now is on display at the local taxidermist's shop, and Mr. Huidekoper's cattle graze undisturbed.

For fifteen years, Mr. Huidekoper says, the demon ravished his cattle, slipping down almost nightly from the mountains to kill a valuable animal. Year after year all efforts to end the wolf's career failed, but a few weeks ago the raider was shot and killed. Since that time no loss of stock has been reported.

Equally noteworthy is the development of the "renegade wolf" phenomenon in the 1920s and 1930s. The "renegade wolf" represented an outlaw, a killer that eluded local stockmen and professional hunters for years, striking fear across a wide area with his livestock depredations. This phenomenon demonstrates how, as the vast number of Montana wolves decreased to only scores, hatred of the wolf produced archetypes. Ranchers named these individuals and endowed them with human characteristics so that the battle against the wolf became a personal one.

The destruction of the "renegade wolf" was inevitable, but in the meantime he became somewhat of a local hero. The phenomenon permitted the declaration of some admiration and remorse for the nearly eradicated species—but only after the wolf had ceased to be the monumental threat that stockmen had been depicting for decades.

The first of the popularized "renegade wolves" worked southeastern Montana. This "Three-legged Scoundrel" terrorized stockmen in the Tongue River Valley for years before Percy Daily shot him near Ashland in March 1920.

Perhaps the most famous outlaw wolf in eastern Montana was the "Custer Wolf," who ranged from Montana into the western Dakotas. He became legendary in his escapes from traps and hunters, and stockmen attributed $25,000 in livestock depredations to him. A newspaper story of his death presents many of the characteristics of the "renegade:"

> The master criminal of the animal world, the Custer Wolf, has at last been killed. The death of the cruelest, the most sagacious, and most successful animal outlaw the range country has ever known was announced with a sigh of relief by the U.S. Department of Agriculture last week. H. P. Williams, the Department's best hunter, sent a bullet crashing through the animal's brain, after trailing it for seven months through eastern Montana and western South Dakota.
>
> For nine years the Custer Wolf struck terror in the hearts of ranchers in that section. Many credited the story that it was not merely a wolf, but a monstrosity of nature—half wolf and half mountain lion—possessing the cruelty of both and the craftiness of Satan himself. . . . He loped through every kind of danger and passed them all. He sniffed at the subtlest poison and passed it by. The most adroitly concealed trap was as clear to him as a mirror in the sun.
>
> Four years ago the Custer Wolf's mate was killed, and it is popularly believed he thereafter devoted himself to revenge for her death. Williams reported that the marauder weighed ninety-eight pounds and measured six feet from tip to tip.

"Snowdrift"—a white male wolf who worked the ranches below the Highwood Mountains in the early 1920s—became Montana's most renowned "renegade wolf." "Lady Snowdrift" was his similarly white-coated mate and, several times, opportunists raided her springtime den to capture their litter. Professionals trained two of the pups, "Lady Silver" and "Trixie," and the pair appeared in a number of Hollywood movies. Another pup, "Lobo," served as Jack Dempsey's camp mascot while he prepared for his 1923 world heavyweight championship fight with Tommy Gibbons in Shelby.

Yet neither "Snowdrift" nor his "Lady" could evade the Biological Survey's trapper Don Stevens. Stevens shot "Lady Snowdrift" in her den only days after local ranchers had captured the eight pups from her last litter to sell commercially. Within a matter of weeks, Stevens set a successful trap for "Snowdrift":

> The wolf was caught in the trap and his struggles broke it from its anchor. For four days, tracked by the government man, the wolf dragged the heavy trap with him and successfully eluded his pursuer. Snowdrift kept to his flight despite the fact that he could not stop to eat, and the heavy trap would have prevented him from hunting any small game.
>
> When Stevens tracked down the wolf, he was able to get within good shooting distance of it, due to its starved condition. He dispatched it quickly.
>
> If Snowdrift . . . had lived in the Black Forest of Germany a few hundred years ago, it would have gone down in legend as one of the most famous wolves of that section, with supernatural powers. During the past years, this wolf is credited with having killed cattle worth more than $30,000.

The "White Wolf of the Judith Basin"—also known as "the Ghost Wolf"—became the last of Montana's "renegade wolves." Because of its color, its sagacity, its livestock depredations, and the relatively late date at which it operated, this wolf's story spread widely. Ample credit also must be given to Elva Wineman, the longtime librarian at Stanford, Montana, who wrote extensively about the "White Wolf" in state and national publications. This renegade often is confused with "Snowdrift," but to the ranchers in the Judith Basin during the late 1920s, no confusion existed: "Snowdrift" had been killed in the Highwoods in 1923; the "White Wolf" had yet to be killed.

The Biological Survey ran a series of expert hunter/trappers at the "White Wolf" during the late 1920s. However, he eluded their poisoned bait, their traps, their dogs, and their rifles. Understandably, with each escape, his fame increased. Stockgrowers from the Highwoods to the Little Belts estimated that they had lost $35,000 worth of cattle, sheep, and horses to the wolf, and became obsessed with his extermination. Hunters who wanted to stalk the legend flooded Stanford with letters. Elva Wineman summarized the situation in an article in the *Denver Post*.

> Aviators want to seek him out with a plane. Men with dogs want to try their skill. A band of Indians has asked permission to come and look for him. A novelist wants to put him into his newest novel. And local stockmen, private citizens, bankers, the postmaster, and others are overworking their typewriters answering letters.
>
> These responses say that, indeed, you must be a good hunter, but we have good hunters here too, and they have failed. And they say that the White Wolf ranges over an immense territory, and that there isn't one chance in a thousand that the letter-writer would have any better success than professional hunters and trappers, who have moved into the country and stayed five or six months at a time, for the express purpose of getting this wolf—and nothing else.

Judith Basin stockmen placed a bounty of $400 on the "White Wolf," but it sat unclaimed into 1930. Then Earl Neill, a surprised local rancher, fired a quick shot at the marauder, wounding him in the left hind leg. However, the legend escaped again. On May 8, 1930, Neill and Al E. Close ran onto the "White Wolf" and chased it into Pig Eye Basin with their dogs. Once the hounds had the wolf cornered, Close drew down on the animal. Then he paused:

> And do you know, I almost didn't shoot. It was the hardest thing I think I ever did. There was a perfect shot, the grandest old devil. . . . I thought swiftly that these were the hills over which he had hunted. I knew that it was the cruel nature of the wilderness—the fight for the survival of the fittest—that made him the ferocious hunter that he was. I thought of all the men who had hunted him, of how his fame had gone out all over the country, and I almost didn't shoot.
>
> Swiftly these things passed through my mind as I stood there with my rifle aimed, finger on the trigger. Then luckily I came to my senses in time and let the bullet fly fairly into the face of the old criminal.

The two men hauled the carcass of the eighteen-year-old "White Wolf" into Stanford, and word of the killing spread quickly through the countryside. All afternoon the streets teemed with curiosity-seekers, many of whom had driven miles into town to witness the legend and to honor Close and Neill.

Close collected the bounty, and friends delivered the carcass to a taxidermist for mounting. The fabled "White Wolf of the Judith Basin" now snarls from within a glass case in the Judith Basin County Courthouse in Stanford. He was six feet long from tip to tip and weighed a gaunt eighty-three pounds. Although recently refurbished, the original taxidermist's job did not do him justice.

The "White Wolf" was not the last wolf killed in Montana, but it served as the last "renegade wolf" of note. For all practical purposes, no "wolf problem" existed in the state after the early 1930s. A population of hundreds of thousands of wolves in 1880 had been eliminated within fifty years. In 1933 the Montana legislature abolished its general bounty on the wolf—although such a bounty remained a county option. Lawmakers agreed that this predator no longer posed a statewide threat to the determined, politically powerful stockgrowers. Between 1883 and 1918, state officials had paid $342,764 in bounties for 80,730 wolves.

After 1930 wolves surfaced in the state only occasionally. These relics had survived in isolated nooks and crannies or had wandered south from Canada. For example, in May 1956 two ranchers killed an eighty-six-pound wolf on Tomato Can Creek, near Nashua in Valley County. Likewise, in November 1978, a rancher found a wolf carcass on rangeland about twenty-five miles north of Glasgow. The Montana Department of Fish, Wildlife and Parks publication *Montana Outdoors* describes the incident.

> This [Glasgow wolf] is the first evidence of a wolf in northeastern Montana since 1956. This particular find is one of only seven wolves handled in Montana in the last fifteen years. Wolves were found in the Sun River area in 1964, 1968, and 1974, near Eureka in 1972, and on the Blackfeet Reservation in 1977.

Authorities included the Montana wolf on the federal list of endangered species in 1973 and on the complementary state list in 1975. Thus the wolf has been afforded complete legal protection from hunters, trappers, and ranchers. Beginning in the 1980s, wolves moved naturally from British Columbia into the valley of the North Fork of the Flathead River, on the west side of Glacier National Park. There breeding pairs established multiple packs.

In 1980 the U.S. Fish and Wildlife Service developed the Northern Rocky Mountains Gray Wolf Recovery Plan—and revised this management policy in 1987. The plan encouraged the recovery of wolves in the Glacier National Park area, in the central Idaho wilderness, and in Yellowstone National Park. This recovery would rely on natural migration in Glacier and Idaho, and upon artificial reintroduction in Yellowstone. Despite livestock-loss compensation programs such as that instituted by the conservation group Defenders of Wildlife, open hostility to the wolf remains.

Professor Bob Ream, who directs the Wolf Ecology Project from the University of Montana's School of Forestry, and some of his students have searched Montana for wolves since 1973. In the process, they have found that Northern Rockies wolf reintroduction, both natural and artificial, regularly engenders opposition from segments of the general public. For example, Montana's U.S. Senator Conrad Burns, in the context of the Recovery Plan, warned that "there'll be a dead child within a year." A Montana rancher added, "They'll want to reintroduce the saber-toothed tiger next."

As wolves return to their Rocky Mountain habitat, their human proponents face strong, rancorous opposition from Montana's livestock industry. For a full century, the state's ranchers have hated, fought, and killed the wolf. Any attempts to return this animal to Montana must face this angry, determined, well-organized force of Montana stockmen.

Hating the wolf is ingrained. It's highly emotional. It's the Montana rancher's heritage. One need not look hard for the answer to the question, "Who's afraid of the big, bad wolf?" He needs only to look at the historical record.

CHAPTER 6

LOUIS RIEL IN MONTANA:
MÉTIS MESSIAH OR TRAITOR?

After more than a century, the name of Louis Riel still produces strong, divergent emotions among Canadians. To some he survives as a visionary Métis hero, while to others he endures as an insane traitor. To most Montanans, the story of Louis Riel remains, at best, hazy and romantic.

In 1869-1870, Riel directed the opposition of the Red River Métis—mixed-blood people of Euroamerican and Indian ancestry—to the new Canadian Confederation government. This insurrection resulted in the establishment of the province of Manitoba and the precedent-setting recognition of civil and property rights for Riel's mixed-blood people. In 1885 he again led the Métis in armed conflict with the Canadian government, this time in what would become Saskatchewan. Because of his participation in the Northwest Rebellion, the federal government tried Riel on charges of high treason and hanged him.

Overlooked in the Riel story is the fact that he spent nearly five years in Montana—the years 1879 to 1884—immediately prior to his return to Saskatchewan to lead the Northwest Rebellion. Those years are most revealing of his past, and are pivotal to the remaining months of his life. Not surprisingly, Riel's activities during his Montana years are interpreted quite differently by various historians. Little middle ground remains.

Was Riel one of the initial spokesmen for French-Catholic separatism? Or was he basically a troublemaker who suffered from wild delusions? Was he one of the first leaders to implement Western Canadian dissent from the federal government? Or was he truly "the John Brown of the Métis," fighting fanatically for social justice? Are both Indians and Métis still suffering because of his misguided leadership? Louis Riel has become a symbol for these various political, religious, and cultural concerns.

In late October 1879, a tall, dark-haired Métis wearing leather clothing and leading two packhorses rode into the Montana-badlands river port of Carroll. This small, crude settlement clung to the south bank of the Missouri River, about thirty miles above the mouth of the Musselshell. Carroll served as the terminus of the Carroll Trail, a freighting road that angled southwest, through central Montana, to Helena. This rough river town became a base for even rougher characters—teamsters, horse thieves, woodcutters, army deserters, buffalo hunters, and wolfers. Because the steamboat season had finished, little activity enlivened the landing in late October.

The rider tied his horses behind the low log building that served as the T. C. Power Company's trading post in Carroll. He entered to trade some buffalo robes with the company agent, Thomas O'Hanlon. In a frontier town like Carroll, no one asked about a man's past for fear of learning too much. Trader O'Hanlon observed this precaution, and it was fortunate that he did because the Métis rider was the notorious Louis Riel, and the story of his life to that point had proved remarkable.

Louis Riel had been born on October 23, 1844, in a Métis farming, freighting, and buffalo-hunting colony in the Red River Valley, in present-day Manitoba. Although Riel always considered himself a traditional Métis, he carried only one-eighth Chippewa blood and seven-eighths French-Canadian blood. He received a rudimentary education in the French-speaking colony and grew into a well-built, handsome, obedient adolescent with a dark complexion, keen, dark

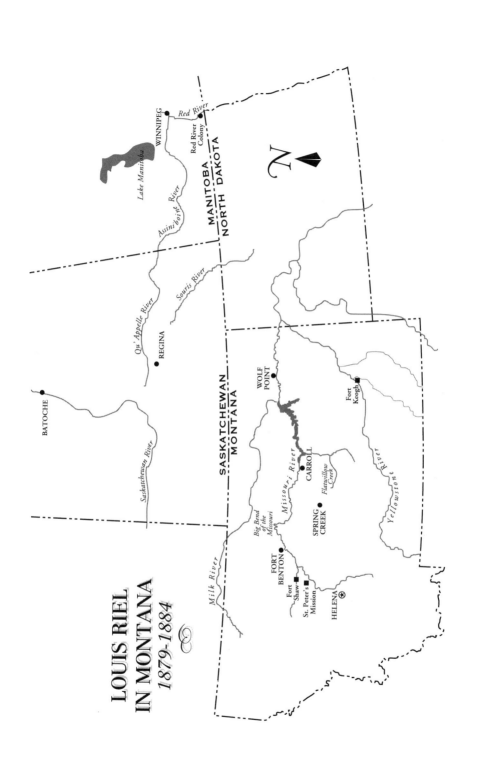

LOUIS RIEL
IN MONTANA
1879-1884

N

BATOCHE

Saskatchewan River

Milk River

SASKATCHEWAN
MONTANA

WOLF
POINT

Big Bend
of the
Missouri

Missouri River

FORT
BENTON

Fort
Shaw

St. Peter's
Mission

HELENA

CARROLL

Flatwillow
Creek

SPRING
CREEK

Fort
Keogh

Yellowstone River

REGINA

Qu'Appelle River

Souris River

Assiniboine River

Lake Manitoba

WINNIPEG

Red River

Red River
Colony

MANITOBA
NORTH DAKOTA

eyes, and thick black hair.

Raised by a staunch Catholic family, the promising youth attracted the attention of the Bishop of St. Boniface, Alexandre-Antonin Tache. In 1858 the bishop sent Louis, then fourteen years old, to be educated at the Jesuit College of Montreal. Bishop Tache intended that the young man would return to the Red River Colony in several years as a missionary, the first Métis priest.

Despite his rudimentary, frontier education, Riel quickly rose to the top of his seminary class. A deeply religious student, he thrived in this environment until the death of his father in 1864 plunged him into months of severe sorrow and depression. Riel quit the College of Montreal in March 1865 at age twenty-one—just months before he would have completed his baccalaureate.

Because Riel believed that he had failed his family, he did not return immediately to the Red River settlement. Rather, he traveled from eastern Canada to Chicago to St. Paul, supporting himself with menial jobs. Not until 1868 did he reappear in the colony—and then only because two years of crop failures threatened the very existence of the family farm. He might have spent the rest of his life in the Red River Colony, as the community's best-educated farmer, had not other forces intervened.

By 1868 the Hudson's Bay Company no longer could control the massive "Prince Rupert's Land," as it had—at least on paper—since 1670. Canadian confederation in 1867 only precipitated the sale of the company's vast lands to the new Dominion of Canada. Yet, in negotiating this land transfer, neither party provided protection for the colony's French Métis, who feared the domination of Protestant Ontario.

In 1869 these French Catholics formed the National Committee of the Red River Métis and elected Louis Riel their secretary. When the committee's pleas for protection elicited no response from Ottawa, it declared a Provisional Government, and Riel became its president.

Under Riel's leadership, the insurgents extracted virtually all of their demands from the Dominion government, while using a minimum of military force. These demands included:

(1) guarantees for preservation of the French language and the Catholic religion;
(2) a land-grant settlement to the Métis, extinguishing the aboriginal land title they had received from their Indian ancestors;
(3) the inclusion of the territory in the Dominion as a self-governing province (Manitoba).

Once these rights had been negotiated, the rebel movement gained political legitimacy, and the local Métis acclaimed Riel a hero. He intended to rule through the Provisional Government until Canadian authority could be established in Manitoba.

However, in March 1870, Riel's government had executed one Thomas Scott, an Ontario Protestant, for leading two unsuccessful uprisings against the Métis state. This execution infuriated the Ontario Protestants, who volunteered by the score for a federal expeditionary force that was sent west to establish the Dominion's control over Manitoba. Riel learned of the force's intention to avenge Scott's death, and he fled Fort Garry just before its arrival in August 1870. Thus the rebel hero became an exile from the very Métis province he had created. The Dominion subsequently banished Riel from the country until 1880.

Between the time that Riel left Manitoba and the day he rode into Carroll, Montana Territory, in October 1879, he experienced a transformation. An intensely religious but proud man—and one recently accustomed to political power—he found himself cut loose to wander. He began to experience visions and revelations, and he gradually perceived himself to be a prophet. He adopted the Old Testament name "David"; he believed that God had chosen him to deliver the Métis people, whom he considered the New World's Israelites.

Early in his period of exile, Riel relied upon his French-Canadian friends in Dakota Territory, Minnesota, and then New England. These supporters were stout Catholics, however, and they found his new religious pronouncements to be heretical. After Riel's actions became more unpredictable, in March 1876, friends surreptitiously committed him to an asylum for the insane in Quebec. Doctors declared Louis "cured" of his delusions of grandeur, when they finally discharged him in January 1878. More likely, he had learned to stifle his pronouncements to gain his freedom.

From this confinement of almost two years, the Métis leader emerged with a plan. He would unite his disillusioned and dispersed people with several Great Plains Indian tribes in a powerful confederacy. This allied force then would invade western Canada and establish an independent republic. From such a self-reliant state, Riel believed that both the Indian bands and the Métis could resist the encroachment of white culture from the east and the south.

The key to Riel's plan was the large Métis population—estimated at more than 7,500—that inhabited Montana Territory and the Canadian Northwest. Because the Métis traded with all of the Indian tribes on the high plains and counted relatives among many of the native bands, they became the obvious catalyst to forge the confederacy. Riel believed that many of the Indians sought just such a solution—especially in the wake of the Battle of the Little Bighorn, which had occurred less than two years earlier, and the attempted flight of the Nez Perce to Canada, even more recent.

In the summer of 1879, having returned to the Red River Valley after leaving New York and a failed love affair, Louis Riel quietly slipped into northern Montana and joined a Métis hunting band. From this base he began to implement his vision. He first negotiated with Sitting Bull's Sioux, Big Bear's Cree, Red Stone's Assiniboine, and Crow Foot's Northern Blackfeet. The talks proved fruitless. Although Riel had become legendary among the Métis, he remained virtually unknown among the Plains tribes. In addition, to native leaders fighting for the very survival of their people and their cultures, Riel's scheme of an independent Canadian state seemed fantastic.

Slowly the Métis leader faced the reality of his failed plan. He settled into a Métis camp of about thirty lodges and, with them, he pursued the rapidly disappearing bison herds on the high plains north of the Missouri River. He soon became the band's spokesman and supplemented its meager existence with his small-scale trading transactions. And that was how he had found his way to Thomas O'Hanlon's post at Carroll during the autumn of 1879.

Louis Riel's presence in Montana had not passed unnoticed by the authorities. They sincerely feared his charismatic personality and his influence among the substantial Métis population. W. L. Lincoln, the reservation agent at Wolf Point, noted on November 15, 1879:

> The Half Breeds are also in force on the Milk River. They have been very importunate in regard to staying in this country, and latterly one Riel (the leader of the trouble in Manitoba in 1869) has acted as their ambassador. He is staying with them, with what object I am unable to say. He can wield the Half Breeds at will, and also probably the Crees.

Despite his reputation, Riel secured permission from the U.S. government for the nomadic Métis to winter along the Big Bend of the Milk River northeast of present-day Malta. The wintering community of more than 150 Métis lodges quickly elected him camp chief.

Riel's extant poetry notebooks—to which he had contributed since his days at the College of Montreal—indicate that, during the winter of 1879-1880, he refocused his divine mission. He abandoned his confederation scheme for a new project: settling the nomadic Métis on a single "reservation" tract in Montana.

After the 1869-1870 Manitoba uprising, many of the Red River

Colony's Métis had forsaken farming, moving west onto the plains of Canada and Montana to pursue the bison herds. Riel found that, because of this change, most of his people had resorted to wandering, hard drinking, and subsistence living. Riel perceived at least part of his mission as securing land title for his people, and thus returning them to farming and a more stable, moral lifestyle.

To this end, the Métis leader rode to Fort Keogh to petition U.S. Army Colonel Nelson A. Miles. He asked Miles to sponsor the establishment of a Métis reservation in southeastern Montana and to request federal funds for the purchase of farm implements, seed grain, and livestock—as well as for the operation of Métis schools. In return, Riel would guarantee that:

(1) all the Métis would obtain valid title to their land claims on the new reserve;
(2) whiskey traders effectively would be banned from the reserve;
(3) the Métis would serve the federal government as intermediaries in negotiations with recalcitrant Montana Indian bands.

In proposing this bargain, Riel requested no more than what the federal government already had granted to native tribes in Montana. During the summer and fall of 1880, to rally support for his plan, he traveled to the major Métis settlements in the territory: Milk River; Fort Benton; Sun River; Helena; Spring Creek (Lewistown). The Montana press publicized his cause, and some editors dramatically labeled him "the John Brown of the Half-breeds."

Again, however, Riel's strategy failed. Colonel Miles held no authority to influence the creation of another reservation in Montana, even were he so inclined. Further, Miles did not consider the Métis potentially useful intermediaries—rather, he thought them complicating agents in an already muddled clash of cultures. Miles noted that most of the Métis remained British subjects, despite their presence in the United States.

Yet even Miles's rejection could not deter Riel. With ever-increased frequency he was experiencing divine revelations. They enforced his beliefs that he was the prophet David and that his mission entailed delivering his people to "the promised land." So Louis focused on the devastating effects that alcohol had produced on the Métis culture: he launched a concerted newspaper campaign to curb the liquor trade on the Montana plains. In a public letter to the *Helena Daily Herald* in 1881, he argued his case for selective prohibition:

> It is a fact that the laws forbid the sale and even the giving away of spirituous liquor to any Half-Breed Indian in the Territory. Another fact is that the laws on that point are not much respected.
>
> The Half-breed is a man who has strong passion for intoxicating drink. He spends most of his earning on whiskey. If he is a mere hunter on the prairie, liquor is one of the principal causes which makes him poor and prevents him from settling. If he is trying to settle, the use of spirituous liquor empties his purse and makes him sink more.
>
> Oh, I would be glad if public opinion would, in some way, take up this matter and help the sheriffs to act against the whiskey suppliers. Those who have the authority ought to stop the shame and force the end of such a disgrace. That is too much degradation!
>
> I invoke the law. I appeal to the moral sense of the people. . . . If the poor Half-breed must be ignored on account of his Indian blood, could he not be taken care of by the law for the sake of the Caucasian blood which circulates in his veins and runs up to his heart?
>
> Let us rather all lawfully keep away from the Half-breeds the de-moralizing effects of intoxicating liquor and help them to progress and to live up to the trainings of both temperance and economy, as a means to attain sooner the other gifts of true civilization.

During the winter of 1880-1881, Riel directed his public campaign for the aggressive enforcement of the liquor traffic laws from a camp of about eighty Métis lodges on Flat Willow Creek, a tributary of the Musselshell River in present-day Petroleum County. He also served the T. C. Power Company agent at Carroll, Thomas O'Hanlon, as an intermediary with area Indian bands. Riel occasionally supplemented his meager income as a woodcutter along the Missouri River and, for a while, operated as a subagent for James Willard Schultz, at that time an independent trader in central Montana.

During that winter, Riel, then thirty-six years old, also courted a local Métis woman: Marguerite, the twenty-one-year-old daughter of the buffalo hunter Jean Monet (also called Bellehumeur). The girl was very dark, timid, self-effacing, and spoke only Cree; she also worshipped Louis. Riel—no stranger to failed love affairs—had become desperately lonely and sought some element of personal stability.

The two Métis were married "prairie style" (without benefit of clergy) on April 28, 1881. The Jesuit missionary from Fort Shaw, Father Joseph Damiani, blessed the marriage on March 9, 1882. Marguerite gave birth to the couple's first child, Jean, near Carroll on May 9, 1882.

Although family life did stabilize Riel's world somewhat, it also brought new responsibilities. The Métis leader never enjoyed an excess of money, and now he worried about providing for his wife and child. In addition, he became embroiled in Montana politics—an arena which, before and since, has ruined men of even greater vision.

In Riel's campaign to curtail the liquor traffic to his people, he filed a lawsuit against another Métis, one Simon Pepin ("the Father of Havre"). The charge involved transacting liquor sales to both Indians and Métis. Pepin then worked for the C. A. Broadwater Company, the chief competitor of the T. C. Power network in north-central Montana. Broadwater's company stood staunchly Democratic in politics, and the Power company proved equally hard-line Republican. Not surprisingly, Riel found support for his suit against Pepin from the Republican U.S. Marshal stationed in Fort Benton, Alexander Botkin.

In return for Botkin's assistance, Riel promised to deliver the Métis vote to the Republican Party in the fall 1882 election. In the sparsely settled Montana Territory—with a total population of fewer than forty thousand in 1880—such a block vote could be most influential. The Métis leader did direct the voting of scores of his people at Carroll and influenced the Métis in other settlements to support Republican candidates. At the time, however, Democrats controlled Montana government. So, when some precincts reported large Republican pluralities, Democratic election officials simply dismissed the votes as fraudulent.

During the winter of 1882-1883, Democratic politicians filed a warrant for Riel's arrest on the charge of complicity in voter fraud. They challenged the declared U.S. citizenship of some of the Métis who had voted. Chouteau County Sheriff John J. Healy, a Democrat, arrested Louis in May 1883, on the Sun River. Although the Fort Benton Republicans bailed him out quickly, the case ran into the spring of 1884, when the court finally dismissed it for lack of evidence.

Louis "David" Riel learned two lessons from his experience in Montana politics: to seek U.S. citizenship for himself and to abandon territorial politics as a means of furthering the Métis cause. Thus, on March 16, 1883, in Helena, Riel renounced his allegiance to the British crown and became a citizen of the United States. In his poetry notebooks, Louis interpreted this act as a commitment to the Montana Métis. At the very least, his Democratic critics no longer could charge that he was a foreign agitator.

Late in the spring of 1883, Riel decided that Montana politics failed to offer an effective means of assisting his people—at least while the Democrats remained in power. Meanwhile, he had assumed an additional responsibility: Marguerite was carrying their second child. Louis realized that he had to abandon the seminomadic life of the Métis bison-hunting camp and provide some economic stability for his family.

As if by divine intervention—and "David" deemed it such—

Father Damiani offered him a position teaching at St. Peter's Mission, south of the Sun River. Riel snatched the opportunity. Although it involved minimal pay, the job would provide his family with a stable home, and he still would be available to assist the Montana Métis.

In late summer 1883, he began instructing two dozen Native American boys in French, English, rudimentary arithmetic, and manual training. When several Ursuline sisters arrived at St. Peter's the next year, Riel assumed control of the entire educational program at the mission. In September 1883, Marguerite gave birth to a daughter, Marie Angelique. Louis seemed to have settled down—as he had not since the Red River Insurrection fourteen years earlier.

At St. Peter's Mission, Riel developed a pattern of work: days of conscientious teaching followed by long nights of writing poetry, crafting religious dissertations, and designing plans for the Métis people. His revelations remained frequent and vivid during his years in Montana. More than ever, he was convinced that God had chosen him to deliver the Métis.

During nights of agitated thinking and writing, Louis concluded that the establishment of a Métis republic in the Canadian Northwest, including portions of current Alberta and Saskatchewan, offered the only solution. This time, with the help of several disgruntled Indian bands, he would make his Manitoba experience work. To his friend, the trader James Willard Schultz, Riel wrote, "Do you know, these people of mine are just as were the children of Israel, a persecuted race deprived of their heritage. But I will wrest justice for them from the tyrant. I will be unto them a second David." Even the long, devastating cold winter of 1882-1883—"the Starvation Winter of the Blackfeet"—could not weaken Riel's resolve. When the killing weather finally broke in March, his premonitions escalated—soon he would be called to lead his people.

On Sunday, June 4, 1884, Riel and his family were attending mass in the small church at St. Peter's when a mounted delegation arrived.

The four Métis—Gabriel Dumont, Moise Ouellette, Michel Dumas, and James Isbister—had ridden almost seven hundred miles from their Saskatchewan settlements with a request: Would Louis return with them and organize the Métis campaign for the redress of grievances against the Canadian government?

Riel replied characteristically, "There are four of you, and you have arrived on the fourth of June. That is a providential coincidence. If I agree, I will tell you tomorrow." Since the delegates sought a fifth person to return with them, Riel recognized the cosmic pattern in replying on the fifth day of June. Of course he would assist his people in Saskatchewan. It was his long-awaited calling.

The Riels needed several days to prepare for the long trek north and for Louis to conclude the spring school term. He told the Jesuit priests at the mission that his trip to Saskatchewan would last only three months and that he would return to teach in the fall. On June 10, 1884, the five horsemen and a Red River cart carrying Marguerite and the children left St. Peter's Mission. "David" Riel, the self-proclaimed savior of the Métis, would never return to Montana.

Once in Batoche—a small Métis settlement on the South Saskatchewan River, about 160 miles north of Regina—Riel worked for several months to unite the various local factions: English Métis, whites, French Métis, and Indians. In 1884 this coalition produced a petition of grievances directed to the Canadian minister of the Interior. It sought the recognition of individual land claims, local representation in governmental affairs, and provincial status for what ultimately would become Saskatchewan. The petition seemed both moderate in tone and reminiscent of the Red River petition of grievances produced by Riel in 1869.

When the Canadian government ignored the request for negotiations, Louis Riel steered the movement in a more radical direction, hinting at armed rebellion. His people proclaimed a Provisional Government on March 19, 1885. The French Métis and the Indians—by then deserted by most of the local white settlers and the

English Métis—again stood in open defiance of the federal government in Ottawa—in what would be called the Northwest Rebellion.

Riel seized this opportunity to proclaim the religious aspects of the revolt. He declared his prophet status under the name "David," and he affirmed God's selection of the Métis as the chosen people of North America. He then established "the Catholic, Apostolic, and Living Church of the New World," and broke his lifelong ties to the Roman Papacy. Riel's vision of a native religious/political state in the Canadian Northwest, refined during his Montana years, finally had become a shaky reality.

The Northwest Rebellion of 1885 proved short-lived. Following several small military victories by the Provisional Government, Ottawa placed an expeditionary force in the field. By mid-May 1885 it had crushed the insurgents. Riel—whose military direction of the rebellion became inexplicably passive—voluntarily surrendered near Batoche on May 15. Officers imprisoned him in Regina and, in July 1885, charged him with high treason against the federal government. His trial began at the end of July.

"David" Riel planned to use his trial as a forum to publicize the Métis grievances and to defend his particular religious vision. In the former instance, he became only minimally successful. In the latter case, the defense team used his pronouncements to argue his innocence by reason of insanity.

On August 1, 1885, following a five-day trial, the jury of six Anglo-Saxon Protestants found Riel guilty of high treason, but recommended clemency. But the law forced the judge to impose the death sentence. After several months of fruitless appeals—some of which emphasized Riel's U.S. citizenship—the authorities hanged Riel in Regina, on November 16, 1885. His mission of deliverance had ended.

To the last moment, Riel perceived himself to be the prophet of the Métis. While imprisoned, he wrote lengthy justifications of his actions in both the Red River Insurrection and the Northwest Rebellion. For the last one hundred years, critics and supporters have argued the merits of Riel's actions and beliefs. Those arguments only intensified during 1985, as Canadians marked the centennial of the Northwest Rebellion.

Frequently lost in the telling of the Riel story is his Montana interlude. The Métis leader's five-year residence in Montana Territory proves absolutely crucial to this story, for it informs both his thought and his actions.

CHAPTER 7

HOGAN'S ARMY

By just about anyone's standards, Jacob Sechler Coxey stood apart—a different sort of fellow. Whether you considered him a crank or a visionary depended upon your perspective. The wealthy Ohio quarry owner certainly had proposed some outlandish programs to Congress. Further, he brazenly had named his son "Legal Tender" Coxey. Maybe he was exactly what his critics charged: "the most dangerous man since the Civil War." Yet, if that were so, why did tens of thousands of Montanans rally to Coxey's cause?

In the early 1890s, Jacob Coxey offered a voice of reform to a most receptive audience. During that Age of Industrialization, popular wisdom held that the federal government existed primarily to assist big business. Yet Coxey's "Good Roads Bill" (1892) asked Congress to ease national unemployment by funding road-building projects and other local improvements that would create jobs. In effect, Coxey argued that the federal government should provide its citizens with the means for self-help. And that *was* a radical idea in the heart of the Gilded Age. Only the agrarian Populists, albeit a valid third-party movement at the time, advocated such progressive solutions to America's problems.

Then, in 1893, a financial crisis struck, devastating the nation's economy. During that year, thousands of factories and businesses closed, while others drastically reduced the number of their employees. In addition, hundreds of banks closed their doors, railroad construction ceased, and dozens of railroads declared bankruptcy and fell into receivership. More than 2.5 million men found themselves without jobs. Many of them roamed the country, hitching rides on freight trains, seeking work. The economic and social dislocation of the Panic of 1893 gripped the entire country, while the administration of President Grover Cleveland failed to respond.

In Montana the national panic hit hard. The Northern Pacific Railroad Company (NP) declared bankruptcy, and the federal court in Helena placed its operations in the hands of receivers. At least a dozen of the state's prominent banks closed. Investment capital for transportation, livestock, and mining projects disappeared overnight.

When the federal government finally reacted to the depression, it repealed (November 1, 1893) the Sherman Silver Purchase Act of 1890—legislation that had sparked scores of silver-mining operations in the state. Immediately, laid-off miners abandoned high-mountain camps to seek work in Montana's cities. Through the winter of 1893-1894, almost twenty thousand unemployed Montanans struggled to survive in a world of few jobs, deflated wages, and no hope of relief.

Into this breach jumped Jacob Coxey with his earlier request to Congress: fund local-improvement programs that will employ the jobless millions across the nation. When rebuffed again by the federal government, Coxey revealed his alternative. Unemployed workers would organize into industrial armies (which he called "commonweals") to form the Commonweal of Christ. These contingents would march on Washington, D.C., during the spring of 1894, to demonstrate their plight.

Coxey believed that his "petition with boots on" would convince Congress of the need for action. He frequently cited the First Amendment right to petition the government for a redress of grievances, in this case on a personal basis.

In the spring of 1894, few Montanans knew Coxey or understood his reform proposals. Yet, to the state's unemployed, any solution

that promised jobs and relief offered possibilities. So in Montana, as elsewhere, Coxey became a symbol of hope to thousands of clerks, teamsters, accountants, railroad workers, lumbermen, salesmen, miners, and day-laborers. In March 1894—about the time that Coxey's own army left Massillon, Ohio, on its four-hundred-mile march to Washington, D.C.—the Montana contingent of the Commonweal Army began to gather in Butte.

Throughout the West, similar armies of the unemployed organized to carry their demands to the nation's capital. From such divergent points as Los Angeles, San Francisco, Portland, Seattle, Spokane, Yakima, and Denver, the tightly knit groups charted their routes across the country. Although they received massive public support and donations for their crusade, all of the armies faced treks of thousands of miles. The transcontinental railroads offered the logical means of travel—from some West Coast locations, railroad companies hauled the Coxeyites either without charge or for nominal fares.

In Butte, by early April, the Montana contingent had formed under the leadership of an out-of-work teamster from the Moulton

Mine, William Hogan. A self-educated, thirty-four-year-old Irishman who liberally quoted Shakespeare, Hogan was of medium height and slim—an unassuming leader. His group of several hundred Coxeyites, soon called "Hogan's Army" by the press, established a camp near the Northern Pacific yards on the flats south of town.

While the Montana army acknowledged Coxey's general program, it emphasized the free coinage of silver at 16-to-1, an obvious reflection of the mining situation in the state. Hogan led not a mob of unruly anarchists, but a well-structured organization of frustrated, determined workers who saw a march on Washington as their last hope of relief. Above all, Montana's "Industrials" committed themselves to a peaceful demonstration, a Constitutionally guaranteed "redress of grievances." By April 12, Hogan's camp had grown to almost five hundred Coxeyites.

Hogan and his two elected lieutenants, William Cunningham and John Edwards, met with the Butte mayor and the Silver Bow County commissioners to arrange train transportation east. The complete support of these public officials reflected the sentiments of their constituents, who daily donated wagonloads of foodstuffs and clothing to the protesters. Nevertheless their request for a special train met with ambiguous replies from Northern Pacific (NP) officials.

The railroad's own situation was confused. During the fall of 1893, the NP had declared bankruptcy. The federal court in Helena had assumed jurisdiction over the company and placed it in the hands of receivers responsible for its operation. So, officially, NP executives could not grant the request of Hogan's "Wealers," even if they were so inclined.

The Northern Pacific receivers watched a rapidly growing camp of Coxey's men beside their yards in Butte, and they panicked. On April 20, 1894, they petitioned federal court judge Hiram Knowles to restrain the Hoganites from hijacking NP property. Such a violation would place the men in contempt of court. Although Judge Knowles ruled in the receivers' behalf, U.S. Marshal William McDermott never personally served the injunction on Hogan. Rather, he wired a telegram to Butte on April 21, which Hogan may or may not have received.

With such widespread support for Hogan's men and their cause in Montana, the Wealers interpreted Marshal McDermott's action as implied noninterference. Butte officials also had concluded that non-interference represented the position of local NP executives. That is, should Hogan and his army commandeer a train in the Butte yards, they would be allowed to run east without opposition. Such unofficial runs had been arranged for other armies of Coxey's crusaders in the West.

Meanwhile, Hogan continued to negotiate transportation with the recalcitrant J. D. Finn, superintendent of the NP's Montana Division, based in Livingston. Again, Hogan's impression of these talks pointed to the railroad's implied noninterference—particularly since mine owners such as Marcus Daly and William Clark had tried to pay for the Commonwealers' special train, and NP executives had refused their offers. Finally, the situation peaked on Monday, April 23, 1894—an occasion in Butte that combined St. George's Day celebrations with Industrial Army speeches and rallies.

Shortly after midnight on Tuesday, April 24, out-of-work railroad men from Hogan's camp entered the NP roundhouse and commandeered Engine #542. They attached a boxcar for their provisions and six coal cars to carry the men. After a short stop at the nearby camp to load, almost 250 Montana Wealers began their trek east, heading for Bismarck, St. Paul, and ultimately Washington, D.C. The Butte dispatcher telegraphed that he had a "wild train" coming down the line—that is, an unscheduled run for which all other trains must clear the track.

The Hogan special sped east and switched onto the NP mainline at Logan, where it picked up about fifty more Industrials. At five-thirty in the morning, the train pulled into Bozeman, greeted by a cheering crowd of hundreds of townsmen. Here Hogan exchanged the coal cars for seven boxcars and coupled on another boxcar full of provisions, donated by the people of Bozeman. With flags flying, the special steamed out shortly after ten, now carrying about four hundred Coxeyites.

The first trouble that Hogan's Army encountered involved a cave-in that covered the tracks near the east end of the Muir Tunnel, between Bozeman and Livingston. After several hours of digging with picks and shovels, the Wealers cleared the rails. The special rolled into Livingston at five o'clock that afternoon, to be met by another enthusiastic crowd.

At the depot, "Lieutenant" William Cunningham climbed atop a boxcar and delivered a rousing speech. The people of Livingston responded with generous donations of food, clothing, and blankets. Meanwhile, Hogan's crew exchanged engines and added a tool car from the NP shops. A raucous, carnival atmosphere prevailed until the train departed at dusk.

Unfortunately, the reliance of Hogan and his lieutenants on implied noninterference proved unfounded. Upon learning that the Montana Army had commandeered Engine #542, U.S. Marshal McDermott ordered Deputy Marshal M. J. Haley to assemble a posse of deputies in Butte and to pursue the Industrials' train with a fistful of contempt-of-court orders.

However, Haley found that popular support for the Wealers flowed so deeply in Butte that he could deputize only eighty men, fifteen of whom deserted before the posse's train could leave town. The *Butte Bystander* characterized the members of this posse as "the scum of Butte." Finally, at six in the morning on Tuesday—fifteen hours after Hogan's men had steamed out—Haley's pursuit train left Butte.

As Hogan's special rolled east, NP Superintendent Finn began his own delaying tactics. Since Finn was already east of Hogan's Army, ahead of the Wealers on the line, he dynamited a rock slide onto the tracks near Livingston. He then spiked switches at Reedpoint and Columbus and drained trackside water tanks to delay the Wealers' progress.

Further, Finn telegraphed Yellowstone County Sheriff James Ramsey in Billings, asking him to stop Hogan's Army there. However, Finn earlier had lost an election to that sheriff, and Ramsey's undersheriff thought the wire a prank. He replied: "COUNTY AT-TORNEY AND SHERIFF OUT IN THE BULL MOUNTAINS, LAYING OUT ADDITIONS TO BILLINGS. EVERY ABLE-BOD-IED MAN IS SELLING REAL ESTATE. STOP COXEY'S ARMY IN LIVINGSTON."

Hogan's 450 Wealers halted east of Livingston and removed the rock slide from the rails—then carefully replaced much of the rubble on the tracks. When they needed water at Reedpoint but found the water tank dry, the Coxeyites filled the boiler using a bucket brigade from the Yellowstone River. On Wednesday morning, they chugged into Columbus and made camp, to the cheers of the townspeople.

While Cunningham was delivering another rousing speech, Marshal Haley's train pulled into Columbus behind the renegade special. Hogan averted a confrontation by ordering his engineer to open the throttle, leaving the deputies standing at trackside. The two trains then raced down the line toward Billings.

At 10:45 Wednesday morning, Billings received Hogan's Army. More than five hundred men, women, and children surrounded the special, while a hundred men climbed into the boxcars to join the crusade. The people of Billings had gathered 400 pounds of beef, 250 loaves of bread, and 400 pounds of potatoes, which they loaded into the provisions cars. Cunningham was addressing the crowd from atop a boxcar when Haley and about two dozen of his deputies approached the crowd from the rear.

To the jeers of the crowd, Haley demanded that Hogan and his men surrender—when suddenly one of the deputies discharged his rifle! In the ensuing melee, about thirty shots were fired. The shots injured several Coxeyites, and they fatally wounded Charles Hardy, a Billings tinner standing on the platform.

The crowd immediately surrounded the Butte deputies and disarmed them. They busted up their rifles on the rails and then chased them back to their train. Cooler heads among the Industrials dissuaded both the crowd and some of Hogan's men from pursuing the frightened lawmen—although Billings officials later detained ten deputies for the shooting of Hardy.

Quickly the Wealers' train crews shoveled in a load of coal and coupled on Engine #464, "the Hog of the Rocky Fork Branch." A subdued army of almost five hundred protesters then switched back onto the mainline to steam down into the NP's Yellowstone Division. Ultimately Hogan's men did gain some time, because the Billings crowd purposefully delayed Haley's departure for another seven hours.

Meanwhile Marshal McDermott and Judge Knowles had wired to President Cleveland, requesting the use of federal troops. Cleveland ordered soldiers at Fort Keogh to intercept Montana's Army of the Commonweal as quickly as possible near Miles City. To this end, Superintendent Finn had pushed his engine down the line to Miles City, to confer with the military.

By Wednesday evening, April 25, Hogan's crusaders had pitched camp at Forsyth, and Colonel John B. Page had issued field rations to six companies of the Twenty-Second U.S. Infantry. Maintaining his pacifistic approach to "the petition with boots on," William Hogan telegraphed down the line that, if faced with federal troops, his Industrialists would offer no resistance. Superintendent Finn received this wire and immediately checked to see if the Wealers had departed their Forsyth camp. When he learned that they had not, he and Colonel Page loaded the troops on an NP special and raced the forty-five miles up the line to Forsyth.

Early in the morning of April 26—two full days after Hogan's Army had commandeered the train in Butte—250 infantrymen surrounded the Industrials' overnight camp. Hogan peacefully surrendered to Colonel Page, although scores of his men escaped into the sagebrush in the dark. Ultimately the soldiers captured about

330 Coxeyites at Forsyth. On Thursday morning, the Montana contingent's dash to Washington officially ended, about 325 miles from where it had begun.

Yet simply stopping Hogan's run and arresting the Industrials did not solve the problem of Coxey's Army in Montana. Federal officers still needed to handle these hundreds of peaceful protesters, in the face of massive public support for their crusade. Furthermore, the authorities faced real difficulty portraying Hogan's men as raving anarchists, bent on rampant violence. One state newspaper reported,

> When Hogan's addition to Coxey's Army was searched at Forsyth, three guns were found. One was broken; one was a .22 caliber; one was made back in the 1860s, for which no cartridges can today be secured.
>
> On the other hand, forty-three copies of the Bible were found. The Army didn't seem to be composed of such desperate characters after all.

Following several days of deliberation, federal officials ordered Hogan and his men to Helena, so Judge Knowles could try them for contempt of court. Three companies of soldiers accompanied the nine boxcars of Wealers in a special train that departed Forsyth at six in the evening on Saturday, April 28, and reached Helena at eight the next morning. Here the men formed ranks at the NP depot and marched out to create a camp at the county fairgrounds. The Montana detachment then numbered 320 men, with about 110 soldiers guarding them. Relations between the two armies remained cordial from their initial encounter. The Industrials even cooked hot meals for the troops.

After a couple of weeks, Judge Knowles's calendar allowed him to address Hogan and his men. He found all of the Wealers guilty of contempt of court for violating his Northern Pacific property injunction, but the sentences varied. William Hogan received six months in the Lewis and Clark County jail; Hogan's engineer and fireman, plus about 40 "officers," earned sixty-day terms; and the other 275 men gained their freedom, after they swore to honor NP property. Judge Knowles dismissed charges against William Cunningham after he testified that he was not really a Coxeyite at all—rather, he was a reporter, hired by the *Anaconda Standard* to cover Hogan's campaign.

By May 20, 1894, the soldiers of the Twenty-Second U.S. Infantry had returned to Fort Keogh, and about two hundred of the freed Coxeyites had established a new camp at the Helena fairgrounds—still determined to reach Washington, D.C. The people of Helena continued to donate substantial amounts of clothing, blankets, and food to the Industrials, but the protesters became eager to restart their pilgrimage. Finally Helena's mayor and the city council devised a plan that would save face for a city caught in the heat of the 1894 "Capital Fight" with Anaconda.

An experienced boat-builder, William Sprague, would be granted a letter of credit and sent to Fort Benton. Here he would direct a small crew of Hoganites in constructing flatboats on which to float down the Missouri River to Omaha, where they could join other Coxey contingents. The Helena Relief Committee for Coxeyites would purchase supplies for the trip, as well as provide five wagons to transport the Wealers' gear from Helena to Fort Benton. So, on May 27, amid much fanfare, about 250 men broke camp, formed ranks, and marched out of Helena behind the wagons, beginning the 130-mile hike to Fort Benton.

Hogan's men straggled into that river town during the next week. Here they found ten large flatboats, bedecked in flags and bunting, as well as a forty-eight-foot cook boat, complete with brick oven and stacks of foodstuffs. The men named eight of the flatboats: *Butte; Helena; Livingston; Bozeman; Great Falls; Free Silver; Hogan; Fort Benton.* Sprague had performed well, and he added considerable capital to the Fort Benton economy.

After some training from seasoned rivermen, almost four hundred Coxeyites pushed off into the bank-high waters of the Missouri on June 6, 1894. The Wealers learned the rudiments of flatboat navigation quickly, for by June 28 the flotilla had reached Yankton, South Dakota. By July 9 it landed even beyond Omaha, at St. Joseph, Missouri. Here the remnants of Hogan's Montana Army joined other Coxeyites working their way east.

In the end, the Coxeyite movement in Montana proved more a harbinger of social change than it did an effective protest. Montana Coxeyism, personified by William Hogan's Army, enjoyed close ties to Populism and to the Rocky Mountain demand for the free coinage of silver at 16-to-1. More important, it recognized human rights over property rights.

Finally, the Coxey movement in Montana emphasized that the federal government must acknowledge workers' concerns and must assume an active role in managing the national economy. Jacob S. Coxey's solutions to the national Panic of 1893 simply surfaced forty years too early: President Franklin D. Roosevelt's New Deal programs incorporated Coxey's ideas to combat the Great Depression in the 1930s.

With the exception of the shooting incident at the Billings depot, the Coxey movement in Montana proved remarkably peaceful—in the best sense, it was a "petition with boots on." It derived from legitimate frustration with an economic system unresponsive to its workers. For that reason, other Montanans widely supported it.

One can argue with William Hogan's tactics, but his concept of a peaceful demonstration to redress grievances finds deep roots in the American heritage. In Montana that demonstration entailed a wild, forty-eight-hour run across the state, which ended alongside the Northern Pacific tracks in Forsyth. This remarkable protest created one of the more curious and instructive incidents in Montana's past.

Chapter 8

THE REMARKABLE PETRIFIED MAN

At the end of the nineteenth century, a phenomenon known as "the Remarkable Petrified Man" surfaced in the backcountry of Montana. This marvel captured the imagination of Montanans because it meshed the bizarre with the scientific—during a social age that easily integrated the two. For example, the Midway Plaissance at the World's Columbian Exposition in Chicago in 1893 had offered scores of unnatural phenomena. Subsequently William Randolph Hearst's *New York Journal* fascinated its readers by emphasizing the extraordinary: the "Great Houdini" and his incredible escapes; the marvels of the ancient Palace of Knossos on Crete; a vast array of animals with two heads.

During the Gilded Age, science had not yet exerted its ahumanistic stranglehold on American popular thought. Thus society adjudged the Petrified Man "remarkable" precisely because he enmeshed the scientific with the extraordinary. Further, he drew reputable Montana civic leaders to his cause as easily as he attracted shady, adventurous characters. This wonder proved to be neither a petrified butterfly nor a petrified top hat. He proved to be much more!

During the summer of 1899, an enterprising young Montanan developed a plan to extract the coins of Yellowstone National Park tourists. Tom Dunbar's scheme involved two horses and a wagon, a wall tent, his camping equipment, and a curiosity. First in the

Mammoth Hot Springs area and then in the Upper Geyser Basin—amid some of the world's most amazing and most publicized *natural* wonders—Dunbar daily exhibited "the Remarkable Petrified Man." Access through the tent flap, into this sanctuary of the extraordinary, cost twenty-five cents for adults and ten cents for wide-eyed children.

In return for this pittance, the intrigued tourist viewed a gray-brown, rocklike form, displayed prone on a makeshift platform of pine boards and sawhorses. He quickly concluded that "the thing" *was* petrified, because Dunbar, in the course of his presentation, "took a club and biffed it over the body with resounding whacks." A reporter for the *Bozeman Chronicle* paid his two bits and emerged with a further description:

> The Petrified Man is 5 feet 8 inches in height and weighs 365 pounds. His hair is perfectly marked, two teeth protrude from the lips, vein markings are visible in the skin, and his hands are tied across the breast with a petrified thong.
>
> One leg is slightly drawn up and part of one foot has been broken off in recovering the fossil from its place of semi-burial. A bullet hole in his forehead indicated the cause of death.

During the late summer of 1899, interest in Dunbar's spectacle spread through Montana's newspaper network. Most newspapermen remained skeptical of the authenticity of "the Remarkable Petrified Man." So to one New York reporter Dunbar explained the origin of this treasure—which, incidentally, was earning thirty-five dollars for him on a busy day.

> Two years ago [1897] I came from the Bitter Root Valley to do some trapping and hunting in the Fort Benton area. One day, in low water, I was working along the Missouri River, a ways below the town. I was looking for tracks and trap sites, when I saw a body half buried in the sand, under the water. It took me most of a morning to get a rope on

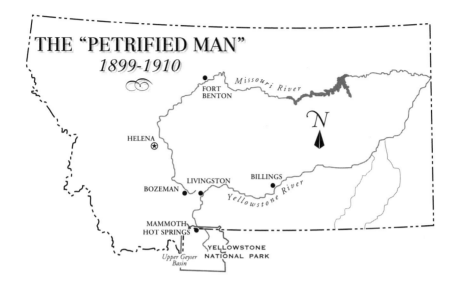

THE "PETRIFIED MAN"
1899-1910

FORT BENTON

Missouri River

N

HELENA

LIVINGSTON
BOZEMAN
BILLINGS

Yellowstone River

MAMMOTH HOT SPRINGS

Upper Geyser Basin

YELLOWSTONE NATIONAL PARK

him and haul him out of the water. That's when the left ankle and the great toe got broken off.

I didn't have a wagon then, so I hauled the body above [the] high water [line] and reburied it in the sand, carefully marking the spot. Then I thought, "As soon as I can get some money to buy an outfit, I'll start a show." And for more than a year and a half I didn't say anything to anybody about him.

Not 'til this spring did I get enough money for a wagon and another horse. And here I am with my Petrified Man. I just wish I knew who he was—when he was alive.

Interest in Dunbar's curiosity continued to run high, and he reportedly refused an offer of $5,000 for the wonder from a visiting count, who wished to ship it back to Europe. In September, however, he sold the Petrified Man to A. W. Miles, a noted Livingston politician and businessman, for what observers believed to be less than one-third of the count's offer.

Arthur Wellington Miles, the nephew of General Nelson A. Miles, had arrived in Montana Territory with the U.S. Army in 1880. He subsequently became engaged in numerous commercial ventures along the Yellowstone River, between the national park and Billings. His operations involved lumber, coal, flour, hardware, real estate, mining, and banking. In 1889 he also erected in Livingston a massive business block, which still stands.

Miles had been one of the original investors in the Wylie Camping Company, formed in 1893, so his interest in Yellowstone Park tourist services was well-established. Along with his demonstrable business acumen, A. W. Miles entertained a strong fascination for questionable speculative ventures. His purchase of "the Remarkable Petrified Man" falls into this category.

Miles added a semblance of humanity to the marvel by placing him in an open pine coffin. Hereafter the Petrified Man traveled in the coffin and often appeared without being removed from the box. In this manner, Miles opened for business in Livingston, in a vacant building near his lumberyard, in October 1899. Townspeople barely could control their enthusiasm and, at twenty-five cents a head, Miles's daily receipts never dipped below sixty dollars.

Miles rapidly developed a plan to capitalize on this local response. He contacted the town's Northern Pacific Railroad physician, Dr. William F. Cogswell—later the executive secretary of the Montana State Board of Health—to examine the specimen. Dr. Cogswell's report became the basis of a widespread publicity campaign, as the *Livingston Enterprise* reported:

> I have examined the body under the lens of a microscope which magnifies eight hundred times, and the nerves and veins could be plainly traced in the particles of formation chipped from the body. The features are clear-cut and natural. So natural, in fact, does the entire body appear that a person knowing him as an animal could not fail to recognize him as a mineral. I would estimate that the man was be-

tween thirty and thirty-five years of age at death.

You have here a rare and nearly perfect specimen of mineral man.

Long may you enjoy his interesting and profitable companionship.

Miles would follow this promotional pattern during his exhibition of the "Remarkable Man" in western Montana and eastern Washington in October 1899. He published the endorsements of Bozeman physicians when the wonder played the Gallatin County Fair, and the testimonials of Butte doctors when the Petrified Man debuted in Silver Bow County. Five Spokane medical men authenticated the curiosity, while it grossed thousands of dollars at the Eastern Washington Fair.

On the return trip, the Petrified Man appeared in Helena, where Dr. Edwin S. Kellogg examined him. Dr. Kellogg worked as the manager and proprietor of the Kellogg Sanitarium, which specialized in the use of "electric baths" and "high-powered X-ray instruments to treat the chronic ailments of women." Dr. Kellogg certified that he had examined the body with "an eighteen-inch-discharge, high-frequency X-ray apparatus." He found its internal organs intact, although "atrofied through petrification." Since no bullet could be discovered in the skull, Dr. Kellogg speculated that the forehead wound had been caused by an arrowhead, which then had dislodged. "Professor" C. H. Gaunt—the manager of the Northern Pacific Railroad's local telegraph office—agreed with Dr. Kellogg's conclusions.

The short western tour proved so financially successful that A. W. Miles then imposed organizational structure on the Petrified Man. In November 1899, with Harry T. Bush (a Jardine mining magnate) and Hugh J. Miller (the Park County Attorney), he formed a stock firm under the name of the Montana Wonder Company.

Local newspapers reported that the Montana Wonder Company issued $26,000 in stock certificates and that eager Montanans purchased the available shares in a flurry. Miles then heightened interest in the Petrified Man by authorizing the Montana Wonder Company to obtain an insurance policy on him. According to its well-publicized terms, the company would collect $5,000 if the marvel were damaged in shipment, stolen, or lost.

Miles, Bush, and Miller then planned an extended trip for their oddity—a tour which they figured would produce their fortunes. The itinerary included towns in eastern Montana and along the Northern Pacific's mainline into St. Paul, followed by a lengthy stay in Chicago. From Illinois the tour would work slowly east, culminating in a triumphant run in New York City.

Throughout the trip the directors planned to employ an advanced-publicity program of newspaper ads, local physicians' endorsements of authenticity, and photo posters. Still, Miles worried. The Petrified Man might represent a one-of-a-kind item in Montana, but the world abounded with similarly unusual phenomena. He needed one additional angle to raise the Petrified Man above the level of the routinely curious.

As Miles pondered this problem, he realized that an Irish miner already had provided him with a solution. When he had displayed the Petrified Man in Butte, this somewhat inebriated miner had approached the casket, gasped, and shouted, "Why, I'll be damned! It's the General, God rest his soul. It's the General!"

"What General?" Miles had asked.

"Why, General Meagher, surely! If that is not the hand of Thomas Francis Meagher, may mine be withered."

Through early December 1899, Montana newspapers discussed the possibility that the Petrified Man could be, in fact, the remains of that renowned Irish patriot, Civil War leader, and acting governor of Montana Territory. The *New York World* summarized the most recurrent versions of Meagher's death. These tales speculated that Meagher either stumbled, dived, or was pushed over the rail of the steamboat *G. A. Thompson*, moored at the Fort Benton levee, on the night of July 1-2, 1867:

For many days cannon were fired, the river was dragged, and the shores and islands were searched. But all to no avail. For the Governor only made it to shore farther downriver. At this point the river was full of islands which swarmed with hostile Indians, not all of whom at that time used gunpowder. The almost noiseless bowstring gave no hint of the shot that cleft his skull.

As we all know, the nerves of the brain work crosswise: the nerves of the left side control the right side of the body, and vice versa. As Meagher's skull was cleft on the left forehead, his right side immediately was paralyzed. The Indians then came and bound the helpless man's hands. Death soon released him from his misery.

Then, alarmed at the commotion made by the friends of the missing man, working their way down the riverbanks, his captors threw the body back into the Missouri. Here it resided until Tom Dunbar found it, thirty years later.

This explanation of the origin of the Petrified Man proved a stroke of promotional genius! Not only could the curiosity tap the legend of a nationally recognized Irish hero, but it also could trade on the still-unsolved, mysterious death of the acting governor. Further, all of the associative speculation would build as the exhibit moved east, toward its destination of New York City—where Meagher had been a most popular, if controversial, figure during the 1850s and the 1860s.

As the exhibit started east, in late December 1899, the directors of the Montana Wonder Company encountered encouraging profits—and one minor scare. When they displayed the Petrified Man in Billings, the aged mountain character "Liver Eating" Johnston and a coterie of his buddies viewed the phenomenon. Johnston, by that time, was nearing the end of a legendary career. A group of his friends were escorting him to the soldier's hospital in Los Angeles, California. They had arranged for his care at this facility, and there he would die the following year.

Paying his two bits and entering the room holding the Petrified

Man, Johnston exclaimed, "Hully gee! I knew that fellow twenty-five years ago. That's Antelope Charley!" As an astonished crowd gathered around him, "Liver Eating" Johnston continued:

Yup, that's my old partner Antelope Charley, as sure as I'm a foot high. We were with a bunch that was working out of Fort Benton, trading whiskey with the Indians for furs. One day I fitted Charley out with ten gallons of whiskey and a wagon, and he went off down the Missouri to collect furs from the wild Piegans. But I told him not to go as far as the twenty-five miles downriver to Eagle Creek, because the Gros Ventres and the Piegans were camped there, and I knew they would kill him.

But Antelope Charley never came back. We made up an expedition to scour the riverbanks, but we didn't find anything but some burned wagonwheel rims at the mouth of Eagle Creek. Now I finally have solved the mystery of his disappearance, one of the last mysteries that was nagging at me. Yup, that's Antelope Charley, right there in the casket.

As this identification of the Petrified Man played through the Montana press, most reporters tended to dismiss Johnston's story, particularly since A. W. Miles increased his publicity linking the stone wonder with Thomas Francis Meagher. After all, "Liver Eating" had reached his mid-seventies, his health was failing, and he was leaving his Montana home, never to return.

More pertinent, by this time many Montanans had developed a proprietary interest in the Petrified Man, whether they fully believed in him or not. They wanted him—like the local grade-school speller—to perform well in the national arena. Obviously his chances of success increased if he were Thomas Francis Meagher. As the *Depuyer Acantha* noted at the time, "People will pay to see a stone man who is General Meagher, when they might not pay to see one who is Antelope Charley."

Miles and his associates worked diligently to squelch "Liver Eating" Johnston's story and proceeded with the eastern tour, publicizing heavily the Thomas Francis Meagher connection. However, the endeavor proved less than financially successful. Only fair attendance characterized the run along the Northern Pacific mainline into St. Paul, and it became truly disappointing in Chicago. Despite a full-page article in the *New York World,* revenue from the New York City showing in January 1900 totaled less than the incurred expenses.

Quietly Montana's Petrified Man had his coffin lid nailed down, and he rode a freight back to Livingston. Miles's worst anticipations had become reality: a phenomenon that could spellbind a local audience and turn handsome profits in the Rocky Mountain West was not sufficiently extraordinary to help Easterners part with their quarters. Likewise the association between the Petrified Man and Thomas Francis Meagher, which carried such legendary weight in Montana, proved too remote for even the Irish in New York society.

A. W. Miles bought out his partners in the Montana Wonder Company and thereafter showed the Petrified Man only sporadically at county fairs in Montana. His publicity barrage declined proportionately. Within several years he lost all interest in the curiosity, and it sat for long periods undisturbed in his Livingston warehouse. Occasionally Miles leased the marvel to an entrepreneur for a showing, but several times failure forced him to wire the freight agent funds to ship the coffin back to Livingston.

For several years, circa 1910, a close business associate of Miles, C. O. Krohne, supervised the exhibition of "the Remarkable Petrified Man." Even after its heyday, Krohne waxed enthusiastically about the profit potential of the oddity. In a letter held by his great-grandson Dwight, C. O. Krohne argued:

> I really believe that it would be one of the greatest money-making schemes anybody could have. I had that man up [in] Yellowstone Park and showed him, and for a week I averaged $75 a day. And I also

showed him at the same time in Bozeman for a week, and I got the same thing there. Then I had him in Bozeman the time the fair was there, and I took in one day $137. . . . Furthermore, I had him down to Billings to the Dry-Farming Convention, and we made very nice money there.

He is the most wondrous thing that people can see, and he "takes" fine after the people see him and start to talk about him. In Bozeman I took all of the professors from the college and let them in free of charge. They took pieces of him and analyzed the same, and they said that he was the real thing. You remember one of his feet is broken off, and you can even see the bone.

Mr. Miles asked $7,000 for him, but I got him down to a reasonable figure. . . . The last price I had from Mr. Miles was $2,500.

C. O. Krohne's optimism, however, could not rekindle widespread interest in the Petrified Man. Finally, just after World War I, an unknown party offered Miles $500 for the phenomenon, and he authorized the sale. Miles's son, Daniel N. Miles, a lifelong resident of Livingston, recalled that he subsequently saw Montana's Petrified Man when the buyer brought him through the state in a trailer. After that tour, the buyer sold him to another showman—and finally even the Miles family lost track of the curiosity's disposition.

Perhaps the Petrified Man still exists out there somewhere. Should he return to Montana, would we greet him with the half-credulity of our ancestors? Or have we become too scientifically sophisticated, too cynical, to entertain such a marvel? If the current "Age of Science and Technology" has extinguished our interest in such sideshow wonders, perhaps we have lost an important part of our cultural heritage.

CHAPTER 9

THE SWAN VALLEY TRAGEDY OF 1908

The front page headline of the *Helena Daily Independent* for October 20, 1908, shrieked: "FATAL BATTLE WITH THE REDSKINS." Three days later, the weekly *Ravalli Republican* wailed: "KILLED BY THE INDIANS." On the same day, the *Kalispell Bee* screamed: "INDIAN LAD SHOT PEYTON; SQUAWS FINISH KILLING." These vivid headlines shocked few Montanans who recalled the clash of Native American and white cultures in nineteenth-century Montana. For, throughout the 1860s and 1870s, Indian-white warfare proved an all-too-frequent event, from battles royal such as the Big Hole and the Little Bighorn to numerous, isolated encounters in which just a few combatants lost their lives.

Yet why did these headlines appear at the relatively late date of 1908? After all, Montana had enjoyed statehood for almost twenty years, and its residents proudly touted their advanced level of "civilization" to prospective settlers. Further, Montana's Native Americans long had been relegated to their six reservations—where they might be destitute and disgruntled but certainly had abandoned open warfare. So what had happened in the Swan Valley of western Montana that recalled Montana's more turbulent days?

On further investigation, the inflammatory headlines presented an incident typical of Indian-white relations in the early twentieth century. The Salish and Kootenai tribes, for example, had occupied the Flathead Indian Reservation for more than half a century, and many of their members had adopted an agrarian lifestyle. The federal government recently had allotted specific parcels of reservation land to tribal members—in anticipation of opening the reservation to white settlement in 1909.

Still, both the Salish and the Kootenai retained some elements of their traditional lifestyles, many of which the Flathead Treaty of 1855 guaranteed. The turn of the century marked a time of transition for these tribal members, a period of meshing old ways with new. It also represented a time when most white Montanans resented any Indian use of nonreservation lands.

One of the provisions of the Flathead Treaty of 1855 guaranteed the Indians' right to use their traditional hunting and fishing grounds, even if those areas lay beyond the existing boundary of the reservation. So each autumn, for decades, small Indian hunting parties had trailed east from the reservation, over the Mission Mountains, to fish and to hunt game in the Clearwater and Swan River Valleys. These hunting trips often lasted from six to eight weeks, and they involved more than tradition. The meat and fish harvested proved critical to the families' winter survival. When hunting in these valleys, the Indians fell under the jurisdiction of the State of Montana. In the Clearwater and the Swan Valleys, Missoula County authorities enforced state laws, and the State Game and Fish warden administered wildlife regulations.

Antoine Stousee and his wife, Mary (49 and 44 years old, respectively), organized just such a traditional hunting party in mid-September 1908. This full-blood Salish family lived on a Crow Creek allotment, south of Ronan. It included a 14-year-old son, Frank, and a 6-year-old daughter, Mary. Another Salish couple agreed to join the party: 46-year-old Camille Paul and his 33-year-old wife, Clarice. At the time, Clarice was a little more than five months pregnant.

Elderly Martin Yellow Mountain and his wife, Sap-Shen-Mah, became the final components of this group. Both of the Yellow

THE SWAN VALLEY TRAGEDY
OCTOBER, 1908

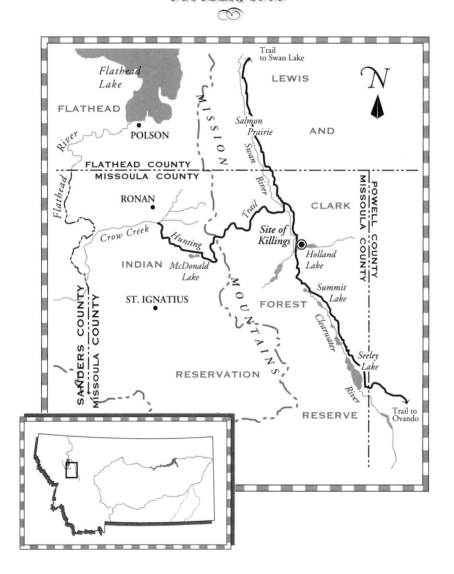

Mountains had reached their late seventies, and age hampered their activities—for example, Martin had lost most of his vision. Still, the old couple yearned for one last hunting trip to the Swan Valley. So the younger men agreed to their request, if Martin would serve as the camp tender and as such haul water, watch the horses, cut wood, and smoke fish and hides.

On September 20, 1908, the party of three men, three women, and two children departed the Stousee place on Crow Creek. They rode eight horses and trailed three colts and nine packhorses, several of which carried their hunting, fishing, trapping, and camp equipment. A few family dogs also accompanied the group. East of Ronan, the party followed a long-established trail that passed McDonald Lake, Moon Lake, and the Frog Lakes before it crossed the reservation boundary through Elk Pass. From the summit of the Mission Mountains, the riders dropped into the Swan River Valley along Elk Creek.

For the next three weeks, the Salish party camped at several traditional tribal campsites along the Swan River, ranging as far north as Salmon Prairie and as far south as Summit Lake. To move camp, they followed a wagon road and a series of trails that today approximate Montana Highway 83, running north from Clearwater Junction to Bigfork. The small party almost daily encountered other groups of reservation Indians, all of whom were catching and smoking fish, hunting deer and elk, and running traplines for small animals. By mid-October, the Stousees, the Pauls, and the Yellow Mountains had located a camp at Holland Prairie, just north of the present-day road off Highway 83 into Holland Lake.

On October 16, their fourth day at this site, Montana Deputy Game and Fish Warden Charles B. Peyton visited the camp. At the time, Antoine Stousee, his son Frank, and Camille Paul were away from camp hunting deer. Peyton told Martin Yellow Mountain and the women that he would return to check the men's licenses and their game.

Charles Peyton was thirty-four years old and had been employed for two years as a deputy by the State Game and Fish Warden. Born in Missouri, Peyton had worked for a number of years as a professional guide in the Bitterroot Valley, using his father's homestead near Corvallis as a base. He and his wife, Linnie, had been married in 1896, and they had three small children. Peyton had been stationed in Ovando with his family. He patrolled the Clearwater and Swan Valleys from there.

According to later reports in the *Missoula Herald*, Peyton "was of very athletic build, enured to hardship, a crack shot, and very rugged, having lived in the open much of his life." The head of Game and Fish, Warden W. F. Scott, further characterized his employee as:

> Pleasant and affable, quiet and unassuming, yet one of the nerviest and gamest men I have ever met. He was one of the most untiring men. His continued rides of from sixty to seventy-five miles a day, over mountains, were remarkable both to me and to the residents of the area.
>
> His vitality was perhaps unequaled, while for bravery I doubt if the man knew what fear meant. . . . As an officer, he was one of the best I have ever known: sympathetic to a degree, yet a terror to evil-doers.

In fact, Peyton's exuberance in enforcing game laws had caused him some trouble during his two-year appointment. Around Ovando he had arrested several longtime ranchers for shooting deer out-of-season. At the time, locals generally accepted such practice if the fellow hunted for food, rather than for sport. Earlier in 1908, Peyton also had cited two state forest rangers in the Swan Valley for exceeding possession limits. Local residents particularly distrusted Peyton because of these arrests.

Further, during the 1907 hunting season, Peyton had been involved in a confrontation with a small party of Salish hunting in the Holland Lake area, as the *Missoula Herald* later reported:

Here Deputy Game Warden Peyton encountered a band of Indians and had trouble with them. He was arresting some bucks for hunting without licenses, when a squaw is said to have jumped in back of him and attempted to stab him with a big knife.

She would have succeeded had not the deputy, just at that moment, turned and caught the force of the blow on the barrel of his rifle, warding it off. The mark remains on the gun today, showing with what force the blow was struck.

This same Charles Peyton, carrying a rifle, returned to the Salish hunting camp on the morning of October 17. Ben Holland, a local rancher, accompanied him. Holland stood by while the warden searched all of the packs and the tepees in the camp. Again Antoine Stousee and Camille Paul were out hunting, but they had left their licenses with their wives. Martin Yellow Mountain also offered his permit from Flathead Agent Sam Bellew, allowing him to travel from the reservation.

That day, the fourteen-year-old Frank Stousee also had remained in camp. Frank had been schooled at the St. Ignatius Mission, and he was the only member of the party who both understood English and spoke English fluently. The young man also produced his license for examination.

That evening Warden Peyton *once again* returned to the hunting camp. On this inspection, Herman Rudolph—a thirty-two-year-old German immigrant who lived in a cabin near Seeley Lake—accompanied him. Rudolph survived as a trapper, ranchhand, prospector, and woodcutter in the Swan–Clearwater area. During the two preceding years, Peyton frequently had deputized Rudolph to accompany him while patrolling the Swan Valley.

On this visit, Antoine Stousee and Camille Paul met Peyton for the first time. Antoine reported shooting two deer, and Camille acknowledged killing three deer and an elk. The young Frank Stousee had shot no game. Peyton informed Camille Paul—who, like Antoine

Stousee, could understand some English but could speak little of it—
that he had filled his quota and no longer could legally hunt.

Again Martin Yellow Mountain presented his permit to travel off
the reservation, but Warden Peyton crumpled it up and threw it to
the ground. Peyton stated that the elderly man was hunting without
a license and that he could arrest him and escort him to the magis-
trate in Missoula. The Salish men, through Frank Stousee, explained
Yellow Mountain's blindness and his role as camp tender. But Peyton
became enraged. He shouted that he held the right to shoot anyone
hunting without a license. Then he stomped from the camp into the
darkness, as Herman Rudolph scurried off behind him.

The three Indian families remained awake most of the night in the
Pauls' tepee, discussing their options. Before dawn, they decided to
strike their camp, load the pack animals, and return to the reservation. However, their departure was delayed somewhat while Antoine
Stousee searched for two of his horses, which had strayed during the
night. Finally, by eight on Sunday morning, October 18, the horses
had been saddled, the packs had been loaded, and the eight Indians
prepared to leave the campsite.

Suddenly, Charles Peyton and Herman Rudolph—both armed with
rifles—appeared from the brush. Peyton entered the campsite and
Rudolph remained at its edge. Camille Paul and Peyton exchanged
harsh words, then shooting erupted.

In just a few minutes, Peyton fell into the snow dead—as did Martin Yellow Mountain, Antoine Stousee, Camille Paul, and Frank
Stousee. The Salish women and six-year-old Mary, as well as Rudolph,
fled to the thick brush. The dogs and all but two of the horses scattered. As the quiet of the forest returned, a fresh snow began falling
over the site of the tragedy.

After the shootout, the native women regrouped. They first laid
out the bodies of their four men, side by side. Then they decided that
the pregnant Clarice Paul should take one of the remaining horses
and get help from any of the other Salish hunting parties in the area.

She would spend the better part of the day, however, before she located the camp of Pascal Hammer and Many Names. Meanwhile, the two other women and little Mary huddled in the woods without a fire, some distance from the campsite.

Not until the next morning, October 19, did the mounted Salish find the cold camp and return to the site of the killings. Everything remained as the women had abandoned it—except that pine boughs had been heaped over Peyton's body and more new snow covered the entire scene.

The Salish men, fearing white reprisals, loaded the bodies of Antoine and Frank Stousee, Camille Paul, and Martin Yellow Mountain on their pack horses. The party trailed some distance from the campsite, where they dug a deep grave and buried all four men together. The Salish men then escorted Mary and Little Mary Stousee, Clarice Paul, and Sap-Shen-Mah back to their hunting camp, where the women spent an uneasy night.

On the next day, the three women and the child began their ride back to the reservation alone. Two contingents of Indian police, detailed to patrol the reservation trails into the Mission Mountains, failed to intercept this party. The women reached the Stousee place on Crow Creek by October 23. Two days later, Agent Sam Bellew brought Clarice Paul and Mary Stousee into Ronan to make a statement concerning the incident. Authorities filed no immediate charges against the two women.

As Clarice Paul had fled the scene of the killings in search of help, so had Herman Rudolph, Peyton's deputized companion. He ran the two miles through the snow to the Holland Ranch, where a rescue party of four white men and two women assembled. Rudolph led them back to the site of the tragedy. Members of the party doubted their right to disturb the shooting scene, and they feared other Salish in the area. So they quickly covered Peyton's body with pine boughs and returned to the ranch. From there, at noon, Rudolph departed on horseback for Ovando, reaching town in the evening. He informed the Missoula County sheriff and the State Game and Fish warden immediately. Almost at once, a posse organized in Ovando to leave for the Swan Valley.

This posse reached the site of the tragedy at about ten in the morning on October 19, shortly after the Salish had removed the bodies of their tribesmen. The group packed out Peyton's body and effects to Ovando, where they turned them over to Warden W. F. Scott. Scott, Rudolph, and several of Peyton's friends accompanied the body by rail to Missoula, where they arrived on October 21.

Peyton's relatives and friends held his funeral in Hamilton two days later, and they buried him in Corvallis. The county coroner scheduled a hearing in Missoula for Monday, October 26, to evaluate the facts in the case and to decide if charges should be filed against the Salish women.

Given the circumstances of the incident, any coroner's jury would run into trouble determining exactly what had happened at that Swan Valley campsite on the morning of October 18, 1908. No one ever will know those events with certainty, because two significantly different versions of the story developed. For more than eighty-five years, controversy has surrounded the shootout.

The first account appeared shortly after the tragedy, in such Montana newspapers as the *Missoula Herald,* the *Helena Daily Independent,* and the *Kalispell Bee.* It reported Herman Rudolph's story:

> After going to the Indian camp on Saturday evening, Charley [Peyton] and I returned to Joe Waldbillig's cabin to spend the night. Charley told Joe that we would go back in the morning and bring those men in, dead or alive, for violating the game laws. On Sunday morning [October 18], Joe loaned me one of his rifles, and Charley and I left early, to get to the camp at sun-up.
>
> When we reached the campsite, Charley told me to stay at its edge and cover him. I was about forty feet from where the Indians and their horses were standing. They had pulled up stakes and had a large quantity

of deer and elk meat packed on their horses, and they were ready to leave.

Peyton walked up to the old Indian [Martin Yellow Mountain] and told him that he was under arrest for hunting without a license and that he was going to take him to Missoula. Then a bulky buck [Camille Paul] stepped out from the group and grabbed Peyton by the throat. But Charley shook him off and told him not to cause any trouble.

As Charley again started for the old man, the bulky Indian uttered a war whoop, pulled his rifle from the scabbard, and was about to shoot at Peyton, when Charley put his rifle to his shoulder and fired, the bullet striking the Indian squarely in the forehead. As he fell, his gun discharged in the air. The two other Indians, who were in sight, by this time had unsheathed their weapons. But, before they could get their guns in action, Peyton killed them both.

When the shooting started, the Indian horses began to stampede. The Indian boy had been hiding behind a couple of these horses and neither Charley nor I had noticed him before. Then I saw him, kneeling on the ground, with a rifle to his shoulder, aiming at Charley. My rifle and his spoke at about the same time.

The lad's aim was true and his bullet struck Peyton in the abdomen, near the navel, cutting through his cartridge belt and inflicting a mortal wound. My bullet also found its mark, and the Indian lad toppled to the ground. I feared that I had not killed him, so I fired another shot into his body.

I heard Charley moaning and, thinking he was badly wounded, I hastened to the Holland Ranch for help. When we returned to the campsite, we found that the squaws had laid out the four Indians' bodies in a row. It was at this time that I discovered that Charley had been shot a second time, in the chest.

We did not know if we should pack out Charley's body, with all the Indians in the area, so I went back to the Holland Ranch and got another horse. Then I rode to Ovando to report the shooting.

Although Herman Rudolph elaborated on this statement during

the next several days, it apparently represents the substance of the testimony that he intended to deliver at the Missoula hearing scheduled for October 26.

The second version of the killings derives from some of the surviving widows and children. Sap-Shen-Mah, the widow of Martin Yellow Mountain, never composed an extant explanation. Mary Stousee and Clarice Paul told their story to Reservation Agent Sam Bellew on October 25, 1908, and they signed the document he prepared that day.

Mary Stousee never added to that statement. However, Mary Stousee Finlay (the six-year-old daughter Mary) wrote a detailed account of the incident in the 1950s, after her mother's death. She said that this piece comprised her mother's story, with some additional information.

Upon the release of this account, Clarice Paul dictated her own version in November 1955 to correct some of the errors that she found in the Stousee/Finlay narrative. Copies of her statement were not released until after her death in the early 1970s. In the light of Herman Rudolph's story, her version of the Swan Valley killings is most revealing:

The warden [Peyton] was to our camp two times before that last night. Both times the men were out hunting. The last night the warden came in the tepee and saw Camille's gun leaning on the pole. He took it and Camille wrestled with him and took his gun back. The warden reached for his pistol and was going to aim, but Camille stopped him, so the warden just stood there for awhile. The other one [the deputized Herman Rudolph] stood by the door, and he asked, "When are you leaving?" Camille said, "You're bothering us. We'll move right away."

The white men stood around and, when they walked out, the mean one [Peyton] said something, but we couldn't hear it. Frank Stousee was standing just outside, and he heard the warden say, "I will come back tomorrow and kill them—shoot them all."

We talked most of the night about when we should move. We decided to wait until morning. Just a little after light, we were all packed up and the horses were ready. I was fixing the girl's [little Mary Stousee's] saddle. That is when we heard the first shot—when we were ready to go and Camille was standing by his horse with his gun in the scabbard, under his arm. The other three guns were leaning against a tree near Frank Stousee. Mrs. Yellow Mountain said that the shot must be a warning, and it wasn't long before we saw the two white men. They came toward us. They were almost in a run.

Mrs. Yellow Mountain was standing by her horse and Martin Yellow Mountain was going to help her on. I was standing by my horse and my husband was fixing his saddle. The game warden came between us and said to Camille, "What are you people going to do?" And Camille answered, "You want us to move and that's what we are going to do. We are going home, over the mountains." The warden shouted, "No! No! No!" and was shaking his head. Then the other warden moved closer, until he was about fifteen feet from the horses.

All the time I was watching this warden that was killed [Peyton], and he was fooling around with his gun. I told Camille, "Look out! He's going to shoot you!" Camille jumped, but it was too late. The warden already shot him. Camille staggered over where we had piled the tepee poles, and that's where he was leaning, against the tepee poles.

When the horses heard the shot, they all scattered except two—my strawberry roan saddle horse and my pinto. Another shot was fired, Mary Stousee and her little girl were running into the thick brush, with Little Mary hanging on her mother's skirt. Then I heard a lot of fast shooting. I looked for Mrs. Yellow Mountain and she was running away too. I saw the mean warden aiming at her, and then she fell down. I thought she was hit too, after I saw her fall.

Then I turned around and went over to my husband. I raised him up, and the blood squirted all over my face. These were his last words, "Run for your life." Then he died, and I laid him down. I turned around just in time to see Antoine Stousee get shot and fall over backwards—near where Martin Yellow Mountain lay, with his head hanging over the pit where he had smoked our deer skins. I saw the son [Frank Stousee] crumpled over on top of his gun. He was shot through the heart and there were bullet holes in his hat.

I started to run towards a big leaning tree. While I was running, I looked back and I saw the warden aiming at me, so I just kept running. I was all braced, because I knew I would be shot at any minute. When I got to this leaning tree, I raised my blanket up over my head and bent to go under the tree. That's when I heard the shot hit the tree above my head. I staggered and fell and then got to my feet again.

The shooting had stopped. So I went back to the camp, and I saw Mary Stousee and her little girl coming back out of the brush too. Martin Yellow Mountain's gun and Antoine Stousee's gun were still leaning against the tree. The warden was shot in the stomach and was sprawled on the ground, but was still moaning.

I went to where my husband was. I looked over to the warden, and he was raised up on one knee. I could see that he was reloading his gun. Camille was lying on his gun, so I raised him up and took his gun from his scabbard and ran toward the warden. The warden did not see me. I ran right up to him, pointed the gun at his chest and pulled the trigger. He fell backward very slowly.

I ran back to where Antoine Stousee fell and checked him. Then Mrs. Yellow Mountain and Mary Stousee and her little girl came up, and I told them the pitiful words, "They are killed. They are all killed." Mary said, "Watch out! The game warden is getting up!"

So I took my husband's gun and reloaded it and ran over to the warden. He was getting ready to shoot us. I ran right up to him, figured out where his heart was and then, almost touching him with the gun, I pulled the trigger. He fell over backwards and yelled. His mouth was open; also his eyes.

I asked Mary Stousee, "Where is the other game warden?" And she pointed and said, "He ran that way." I made a circle in the trees, looking for him, but I could not find him, so I came back to the camp.

The first thing we did was lay out our men's bodies in the old way. There were only my two horses left. Mrs. Yellow Mountain told me to take a horse and get help, because I knew where the Flathead camps were. I took my roan and started out on a gallop down the trail. I had trouble finding help, but finally I did find help.

Clarice Paul's account, suppressed for more than sixty years, continues. It addresses the return of the native women to the campsite, the burial of their men, and their four-day trek back to the reservation through the snow.

With Mary Stousee, Clarice had provided a much-abbreviated version to Agent Bellew on October 25, 1908. Yet their description of the encounter received little exposure in Montana newspapers. Only "Z," an anonymous, reservation-based correspondent, told the conflicting account in the *Daily Missoulian* and the *Kalispell Bee*. Furthermore, this story appeared almost one week after the scheduled hearing in Missoula.

That hearing proved anticlimactic. When it convened on Monday morning, October 26, county officials disclosed that the preliminary evidence gathered by Agent Bellew—including the abbreviated statement of Clarice Paul and Mary Stousee—had disappeared from the Missoula County Attorney's Office. More important, Herman Rudolph did not appear at the hearing. He had frequented a number of Missoula bars during the weekend, telling his story and being feted as a local hero. Yet, when Monday morning arrived, Rudolph could not be found. No one ever saw him again in western Montana. The hearing produced no recommendations for prosecution.

C. Hart Merriam, the renowned naturalist, coincidentally was visiting the Flathead Reservation in late October, to examine the boundaries for the proposed National Bison Range near Ravalli. He conducted his own investigation of the incident and published a pro-Indian version in the widely distributed periodical *Forest and Stream*. This exposure brought national pressure on Agent Bellew's successor,

Fred C. Morgan, to pursue the issue on behalf of the Salish widows and children.

Between 1909 and 1915, Agent Morgan repeatedly requested an investigation by the Missoula County Attorney's Office, since the killings fell under its jurisdiction. At one point he forwarded his only copy of the complete federal file on the dispute to the County Attorney's Office—where it promptly was "mislaid" and never recorded.

If some national sympathy evolved for the native side of this encounter, strong public opinion in western Montana continued to support Peyton's actions. In the Eleventh Montana Legislature, which convened early in 1909, supporters introduced *Senate Bill 19*: "An act for the relief of the widow and minor children of Charles B. Peyton, a Deputy State Game Warden, who was killed by Indians while in the performance of his official duty on October 18, 1908." This bill sought a lump-sum payment of $5,000 to the Peytons from public funds.

As the Senate Committee on Finance and Claims heard testimony concerning the incident, however, sponsors quietly tabled the bill. In its place appeared *House Joint Resolution 13*, which recommended that the Montana State Game and Fish warden appoint Mrs. Linnie Peyton a deputy warden for a four-year term, at an annual salary of $1,500. Since the state warden never authorized that appointment, this resolution simply enabled the legislature to save face, at no public expense.

In the end, authorities made neither a monetary nor a legal decision concerning the Swan Valley tragedy. Peyton's widow and three children remained uncompensated. The state never paid reparations to Sap-Shen-Mah Yellow Mountain, to Mary Stousee and her daughter, or to Clarice Paul and her son, John Peter, who was born in mid-January 1909. Neither county, nor state, nor federal officials ever filed formal charges against any party in the incident.

This isolated violent encounter continues to live in the popular history of Montana. Sometimes the story is told from the Peyton perspective, and other times it is related from the Indian position. The extant evidence, because of its contradictory nature, requires that each of us decides who bears the responsibility for this tragedy. Or was the 1908 Swan Valley tragedy an inevitable product of Montana's clash of cultures?

CHAPTER 10

CARRY NATION VS. BUTTE, AMERICA

P rohibition crusader Carry A. Nation stepped off the Northern Pacific mainliner into cold darkness at Butte's Front Street depot just before five in the morning on Tuesday, January 25, 1910. She had traveled from Arkansas to confront evil in America's most morally corrupt community. After one day in the mining town, she would assert,

> I have never seen a town as wide open as Butte! I have never seen so many broken hearts! I have never seen so many homes consumed to keep up the saloon! If I could touch a button and blow all the saloons in Butte to hell, I would do it in a minute. . . . I'm talking to the bosses of this town, the rulers of this town, now. I'm talking to the voters. I have brought you a remedy—God's remedy!!

The fiery reformer had selected a formidable opponent—Butte boasted more than 275 saloons, and scores of other dens of iniquity. Even the city's mayor, Charlie Nevin, owned a saloon. By 1910, when Carry Nation reached the height of her short-lived career, Butte had established itself as a town of readily available vice. The confrontation would test the mettle of both parties.

With the furor of a Kansas tornado, Carry Nation had roared onto the popular American scene a decade earlier, on December 27, 1900. At eight o'clock that morning, she swept into Wichita's most renowned, elegant watering hole, the Hotel Carey Annex. She set her formidable jaw and carried the fire of the righteous in her eyes. Mrs. Nation shrouded her muscular, five-foot ten-inch, 175-pound frame in a floor-length black cape. The garment also concealed her weapons of destruction: a one-foot iron rod; an assortment of carefully selected rocks; and a four-foot cane with an iron ring strapped to the end.

During the next twenty-five minutes, the fifty-four-year-old whirlwind smashed and whacked and splintered, and wreaked about $3,000 in damage. Her prime targets included a long sideboard, an exquisite Venetian mirror, a crystal chandelier, and a heretofore undistinguished, but enormous, painting of sylvan nudes entitled *Cleopatra at the Bath*. With this attack, Carry Nation, the self-proclaimed smashing reformer, began her frenetic mission.

Carry Amelia Moore was born in Kentucky in 1846. Although her family moved a dozen times within Kentucky and to Texas and Missouri during her childhood, she received a better-than-average education. In 1867 she married Dr. Charles Gloyd—a physician, Union Army veteran, and alcoholic. Unable to reform him, Carry and her daughter deserted Dr. Gloyd; shortly thereafter he died.

Ten years later, Carry married David Nation, a minister, lawyer, and editor who was nearly twenty years her senior. In 1899 the family lived near the border of Oklahoma Territory, in Medicine Lodge, Kansas, where David Nation served the town's First Christian Church congregation. There Carry organized a county chapter of the Woman's Christian Temperance Union (WCTU) to combat what she perceived as rampant alcoholism in a state that legally had been "dry"—devoid of alcohol—for almost two decades.

While living in Medicine Lodge, Carry started to receive frequent visions commanding her to attack evil and its perpetrators in their lairs. The cosmic advice directed her to battle not only Satanic

CARRY NATION'S
MONTANA TOUR
JANUARY 24-FEBRUARY 10, 1910

substances, but also the businesses hawking those substances: not just alcohol, but saloons; not just tobacco, but cigar shops; not just illicit sex, but brothels.

A particularly graphic "vision" had driven Mrs. Nation to Wichita and to the Carey Hotel Annex. They would compel her, during the next ten years, to lecture and smash from one American coast to the other, through Canada, and to Great Britain. Finally they would drive the furious activist to embark for Montana, to offer salvation to the people of Butte, a city reputed to be the most vice-ridden town in America.

Between 1900 and 1910, Carry Nation became the country's most visible prohibition figure. The American press gloried in reporting "The Smasher's" every violent act and her every extreme statement, as well as her divorce from the Reverend Nation. She assumed a hardware-store hatchet as the symbol of her campaign. She sold miniature hatchet replicas to members of her audiences, to supplement her lecture fees.

With the income from these tours, Carry established a "Home for the Wives of Drunkards" in Kansas City. She also published two prohibition newspapers, first *The Smasher's Mail* and then *The Hatchet*. These same revenues paid her bail and fines. That proved important, for authorities jailed her more than thirty times during the decade—seven times alone in Topeka, Kansas! The charges ranged from disturbing the peace to malicious assault to inciting to riot. The rest of her income Carry plowed back into her divine crusade.

Early in 1910, America's apostle of violent reform again needed some capital for her temperance projects. Once again her "visions" responded to the call. They commanded Mrs. Nation to carry the message of truth and salvation to the flamboyant copper-mining town of Butte, Montana—or, as she called it, "America's cesspool of alcohol, tobacco, and sinful women."

In response, the crusader contacted a number of WCTU chapters in Montana and received favorable replies from ten of them. She then scheduled a two-week campaign to begin in Montana's moral hellhole on January 25. Besides Butte, the tour would include Anaconda, Missoula, Stevensville, Hamilton, Helena, Bozeman, Livingston, Laurel, and Billings. But Butte remained Carry's real target.

In 1910, the city of Butte was the hub of mining operations in a mining state. It sported a population of almost fifty thousand, Montana's largest urban concentration. Activity flourished there twenty-four hours a day because of the mines' continuous shifts. Butte's inhabitants were predominantly single, male, foreign-born miners. The town's business community catered openly to this clientele. Butte also functioned as a staunch union town, although controlled by the Amalgamated (Anaconda) Copper Company. It had survived the "War of the Copper Kings" among Marcus Daly, William A. Clark, and Fritz Heinze, and it was surviving the reign of the Standard Oil Company. It was a wide-open town, a rough town, a laborer's town, an exciting town in which to live.

Butte also remained a community of incongruities: it could afford to import the nation's best actors and songbirds from New York City, yet its "restricted district" was notorious throughout the West; it could support 4 daily and 5 weekly newspapers and 38 recognized religious congregations, yet more than 275 saloons operated there.

When Carry Nation stepped onto the Northern Pacific platform on January 25, she met Mrs. W. E. Currah, the president of the Butte chapter of the WCTU. Mrs. Currah whisked Carry through the predawn darkness to the guest bedroom of her home on Fremont Street. From bed, the sixty-three-year-old Mrs. Nation granted her first interview four hours later—clad in her gold-rimmed spectacles, a plain cotton dressing gown, and a gray shawl. To the *Butte Inter Mountain* reporter, who must have anticipated a wiry, possessed demon, she presented a surprising figure:

> Why, she might be anybody's grandmother, with those soft wrinkles— a remarkably good face, despite the piercing eyes of almost the same shade as the dull gray hair that fell loosely over her shoulders and also despite the slightly protruding underjaw which snaps sharp against the upper as she drives home her pithy, biting arguments. Her teeth come together much as do Colonel Teddy Roosevelt's. It suggests power and partially explains her stunts with the hatchet.

Bending forward to punctuate her statement, Carry outlined her plan of assault on sin in Butte. She would speak in the evenings at the Mountain View Church, the Grace Methodist Episcopal Church, and the Shortridge Christian Memorial Church, on a rotating basis. She also would talk to the assembled members of the Butte Bartenders' Union, if they would invite her to the meeting hall. If they would not, she would visit as many saloons or "joints" as possible, to persuade their owners and barkeeps to close them permanently. Further, she would tour Butte's famous red-light district.

When the reporter suggested that a trip to the "tenderloin" might be futile, she seized the opening, responding, "No! I must go to see the harlots too. They are poor, miserable creatures. Their lot only shows what vice mixed with drink will do. They live daily with the thought, the hope, of suicide. That is their only release."

Thus reprimanded, the newspaperman apologized. Then Mrs. Nation, ever aware of the value of good public relations, reached for her oversized carpetbag to award him a souvenir temperance pin. A New Jersey supplier mass-produced these trinkets for the crusader, and she sold them for $1 apiece following her lectures. The pin comprised a little gold-plated hatchet, with a mother-of-pearl blade and an imitation diamond inset. Down the handle ran the engraved legend "Carry A Nation." The matron, not immodestly, explained its significance.

> That's the movement. I don't expect to Carry *the* Nation, but it's being done. The temperance movement is gaining ground everywhere, and in Montana too. We may not win this year, but we will next year. My name, you see, is not an accident. Carry A Nation—that's it!

The morning interview, or sermonette, ended with the reformer issuing a veiled threat to engage in some saloon smashing—which she commonly called "hatchetation"—in Butte.

Immediately members of the Butte Bartenders' Union became embroiled in an internal battle over whether to permit Carry to address their assembly. After much public discussion, they decided against granting her an audience. Thus she spent much of her time between speaking engagements by visiting individual bars and learning the layout of Butte's "tenderloin" district.

For her Butte lectures, Carry Nation invariably packed the house. Both her followers and her detractors agreed that she possessed the greatest stage presence of any woman who had performed in the city. The *Butte Miner* reported,

> On the platform she is clever. She has a rapid-fire method of delivery that carries her arguments home and a sense of humor that

saves her from being prosy. Mrs. Nation speaks as if she were sincere, as if her methods of attack were consecrated—as she says they are. But her slam-bang sort of oratory leaves no phase of the traffic she is attacking without its marks of excoriation.

The Smasher's performances typically incorporated praying, hymn singing, temperance slogan-chanting, and preaching against the world's evident, immediate evils. By 1910 her list of these evils had grown to impressive length. One reporter wrote:

> Mrs. Nation's energetic presentation, entitled "Why I Use the Hatchet," was a sermon interspersed with stories and morals. During the course of the two-hour tirade, she traveled from gin to perdition and all the way back again. Mrs. Nation denounced, in smashing terms, the following: saloon keepers; tobacco users; gamblers; scarlet women; women who wear "rats" [small coiffure pads]; Merry Widow hats; President William Howard Taft; former President Theodore Roosevelt; the Masonic fraternity; the Unitarian Church; the Christian Science Church; quack doctors; women who wear anything but plain dress and modest attire; the Republican Party; the Democratic Party; the Socialist Party; the Anti-Saloon League. In short, she scored everybody who does not endorse her brand of prohibition, and then some others!

The lectures also included frequent references to her autobiography, entitled *The Use and Need of the Life of Carry A. Nation*, which had been published in 1909. When she concluded the performance, Carry the possessed reformer became Carry the possessed huckster. The *Butte Inter Mountain* noted that "her manner of selling would do shame to the best auctioneer on earth," since she shouted to the crowd, "Those who want my book and my hatchet pins step right up here quick! Those who don't, get right out! You want two, three, all right? Three dollars! Come right along. Step lively!"

The crusader consistently enjoyed a lucrative business following her Butte lectures, grossing from $225 to $300 each evening. She usually charged no admission fee to the lectures, and donated one-third of these revenues to the host churches and to the local chapter of the WCTU to cover their costs.

One evening, following a particularly robust delivery at the Grace Methodist Episcopal Church in South Butte, Carry hawked her wares. Then, responding to a recent "vision," she led a march of more than five hundred supporters toward Butte's "tenderloin" in the Fifth Ward. Clutching her Bible and clad in a plain dark cape and a black poke-bonnet, the crusader strode through the chilly night.

Many of Mrs. Nation's followers wore the white ribbons of the WCTU or the armbands of the Salvation Army. All of the marchers joined in singing the battle hymns of the temperance movement. The anticipated confrontation with the vile sins of the Butte under-world would occur!

As she approached the ABC Dance Hall on South Wyoming Street, the crowd swelled to more than one thousand persons—including many jeering critics and curiosity seekers. Once Mrs. Nation had forced her way through the doors of the ABC, she accosted a group of men seated at tables near the bar. In a fiery attack she assured them that they occupied a place lower on degradation's scale than did the women who "rustled" there. Then she turned her wrath on the bar-tender. He raised his towel in defense and shouted a warning to her that he had summoned a policeman to eject her. The crusader replied,

> Would you call an officer to arrest a defenseless, gray-haired old woman? What are you afraid of? Your mother was a woman. Would you call an officer to arrest her? What would she say if she knew you were behind a bar, selling the drink that damns men's souls and sends them to hell? She never raised you to consort with these lewd, bawdy, and unfortu-nate creatures or to be surrounded by this appalling vice and by all the wiles of Satan.

Honor your mother, my good man! Close this saloon down!

The embarrassed, befuddled barkeep pleaded in reply, "For God's sake, woman, get out of here."

To this The Smasher rejoined, "I will not! It is precisely for God's sake that I came in here!" However, she then did turn and push her way through the crowd, leaving the ABC as the band struck up "What the Hell Do We Care."

Once again on the street, Mrs. Nation led the faithful and the decriers to the ABC's terraces of cribs. She entered each door not locked by its female occupant and spoke individually to its inmate. She received no abuse from the girls. To each she delivered virtually the same speech in a passionate, almost tearful voice—as one would use with a wayward child:

Leave this hell hole, my dear, this life of shame. You have a mother. What would she say if she knew you were here? This life leads to but one thing—an early unwept grave—for the wages of sin are death. Leave it! Leave it! For you are still young, and not beyond redemption.

The men who come here nightly to appease their passions and to flatter you haven't the respect for you that they show a dog. They talk worse of you than they do of dogs! They curse you and they hate you, for they are ashamed. Oh, my girl, leave this life while you may. It is hell here below, and it is hell hereafter.

Not waiting for immediate converts, the stocky crusader forced herself through the now-unruly crowd and preceded them up Wyoming Street to the Copper King's boardwalk. At this saloon—with accompanying rooms—she tried to deliver an impromptu sermon in the cold half-light. The *Butte Miner's* reporter assigned to the confrontation captured the street scene:

It was an odd spectacle. Prostitutes with painted cheeks, heavy red lips, and leering eyes that betokened too much drink, and in scant attire, mingled with WCTU matrons, and rowdies, and the curious. Mrs. Nation was subjected to shouted abuse and insult most vile. And the French and the colored women cursed her and jostled her.

Bare heads, shoulders, and arms were thrust out of half-closed doors. Women in attire which was sans skirts and sans most everything else flocked to the scene and, shivering, they leered, jeered, and hooted at Mrs. Nation. The din soon became deafening.

Unable to command the crowd, the fiery radical stomped off, picking her way down Galena Street, though a narrow passageway, and onto Mercury Street, with the mob surging behind her. She knew her next target, and she entered the Windsor Saloon straightaway. Pushing into the dance hall, Carry gestured at the paintings of nude women on the walls and shrieked, "See those? It's a shame and a disgrace! Those lewd, indecent pictures are there to arouse the lust in man!" She then commenced a short discourse on intemperance and on the folly of the primrose path.

Just as Carry concluded, the bartender entered the room and ordered the orchestra to play. So the crusade retreated to the front door. Here the owner, the comely May Malloy, accosted her. Screaming obscenities, the young woman attempted to encircle Carry's ample waist and to wrestle her through the door. In the process, May tore her opponent's bonnet from her head and wrenched her arm. For good measure, in parting, the owner administered a well-placed kick. The crowd outside immediately fell silent, unnerved by this turn of events.

The heretofore indomitable activist of the Prohibition movement had been stymied. Indeed, Butte had proved something more than a worthy adversary. Carry slipped through the milling, hushed crowd, down a darkened alley, and alone walked through the night to the Currah house on Fremont Street. The Smasher had engaged in no smashing in Butte; she would do no smashing in Montana.

Carry Nation remained in Butte for several more days, lecturing to sympathetic audiences—including the assembled Butte Newsboys' Club—and visiting Columbia Gardens and the municipal police court. However, her white-hot fire of indignant righteousness had paled. In fact, the remainder of her Montana tour proved anticlimactic. Even a saloon keeper on Front Street in Missoula, who had erected a banner proclaiming free "Carry Nation Cocktails" in mocking honor of her visit, incurred only a knee-jerk response from the gray-haired radical.

On February 10, 1910, Carry Nation boarded the Northern Pacific mainliner in Billings, after concluding a presentation at the Baptist Church. She steamed off in the direction of South Dakota to rally prohibition forces there, prior to an April election on the issue. A little more than one year later Mrs. Nation died in Leavenworth, Kansas, accompanied only by the demons and dragons and imps of her "visions." Thus the short-lived crusade of one of America's most flamboyant and indiscriminate reformers ended.

Carry Nation had confronted the forces of evil in their most inner sanctum—Butte, America. Yet she had not emerged victorious. Montana would adopt a statewide prohibition law in 1916, but that resulted more from the firm, continuous persuasion of local members of the WCTU, the Anti-Saloon League, the Salvation Army, and the suffrage movement than from her efforts. As the *Livingston Enterprise* noted upon Carry's departure from Montana in 1910:

Carry Nation came to Montana. She saw, but she failed to conquer. The visit of this celebrated person to the state did no harm—and possibly it did no good. But the people here were glad to see her. And she is welcome to come back and try again. For there is room for improvement here.

CHAPTER 11

IMPEACHING JUDGE CRUM

O nly twice in Montana's history has a state official been impeached and banished from office. In 1918 the Montana Senate removed Judge Charles L. Crum from the bench of the Fifteenth Judicial District; in 1927 that same body deposed T. C. Stewart as Secretary of State. In the earlier instance, the impeachment devastated the life of an able, principled jurist. However, that impeachment reflected the nature of Montana during World War I.

By the time the United States formally declared war on Germany on April 6, 1917, Montana and the nation had been involved emotionally in "the European war" for more than two years. Most Montanans, although officially neutral, supported Great Britain and its allies—particularly after the sinking of the *Lusitania* in May, 1915. By early 1917, a peculiar kind of war hysteria gradually had spread across Montana and infected many of its citizens. Very much like the Spanish Influenza epidemic that would sweep the state at the end of the war, this pro-American fanaticism started slowly and built quietly, but ultimately reached crisis levels in many Montana communities.

The fervor with which many Montanans supported German-bashing on the home front, in the name of the American war effort, remains difficult to comprehend. Yet the war years in Montana proved a frightening time for residents of German ancestry, for citizens suspected of pro-German sympathies, for any of the foreign-born, for Montanans who did not embrace the war hysteria, and for anyone who opposed the wholesale suspension of Constitutionally guaranteed civil liberties.

Once the United States declared war on Germany—despite the vote of Montana's Jeannette Rankin and fifty-five other members of Congress—Montana jumped in with both feet. Almost forty thousand persons, or ten per cent of the population, either enlisted or were drafted. Thus Montana made a greater per capita contribution to the manpower pool than any other state in the nation. Montana farmers borrowed money in massive amounts to expand their acreage and produce bumper crops. Liberty Bond drives and Red Cross subscriptions across the state regularly exceeded their goals. The Butte–Anaconda copper industry worked continuous shifts, seven days a week, to set production records.

Within the state, the Montana Council of Defense (MCD) coordinated the war effort. Early in 1917, Governor Samuel V. Stewart created this Montana group with the encouragement of President Woodrow Wilson and the Council of National Defense. The MCD, with Governor Stewart sitting as *ex officio* chairman, immediately established county and community councils, extending its quasi-legal authority to them.

Initially the MCD worked to increase agricultural production, to organize patriotic Liberty Leagues, to encourage enlistment in the military, and to promote Liberty Bond and Red Cross drives. By the summer of 1917, however, zealous members of the state and the local councils turned to more insidious tasks. They began to identify and harass "slackers" and other fellow citizens suspected of holding pro-German sympathies or having contributed too little to patriotic subscriptions. "Work, War, or Jail!" became the rallying cry of the Council.

Rapidly Montanans crossed the line of appropriate patriotism and

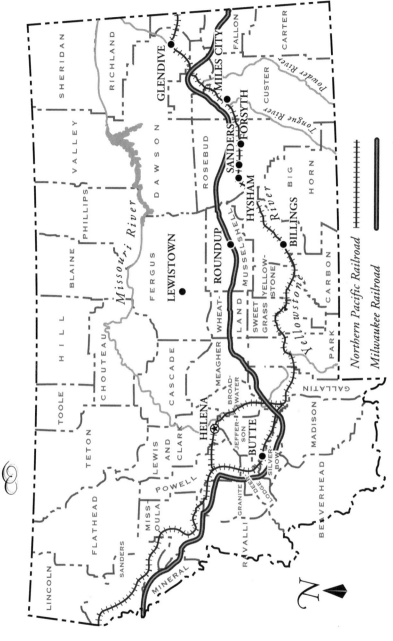

MONTANA'S COUNTIES
1918

Northern Pacific Railroad

Milwaukee Railroad

LINCOLN

FLATHEAD

SANDERS

MISSOULA

MINERAL

LEWIS AND CLARK

POWELL

RAVALLI

GRANITE

DEER LODGE

SILVER BOW

BUTTE

JEFFERSON

BROAD-WATER

MEAGHER

HELENA

BEAVERHEAD

MADISON

GALLATIN

PARK

CARBON

BILLINGS

BIG HORN

YELLOWSTONE

SWEET GRASS

WHEAT-LAND

MUSSELSHELL

ROUNDUP

HYSHAM

SANDERS

FORSYTH

ROSEBUD

CUSTER

CARTER

FALLON

MILES CITY

GLENDIVE

DAWSON

FERGUS

LEWISTOWN

CASCADE

CHOUTEAU

TETON

TOOLE

HILL

BLAINE

PHILLIPS

VALLEY

RICHLAND

SHERIDAN

Missouri River

Yellowstone River

Tongue River

Powder River

began attacks on "un-American activities." Billings sported an active, self-appointed "Third Degree Committee" to handle local noncon-formists. A Glendive contingent nearly lynched a local German Mennonite minister because of his pacifist beliefs. A Lewistown mob raided the Fergus County High School for German books, then burned them at a downtown rally. Overzealous patriots dragged hun-dreds of their neighbors before public assemblies and forced them to document their Liberty Bond purchases or demonstrate their patrio-tism by kissing the American flag and reciting the Pledge of Alle-giance.

Given this rampant irrationality, well-intentioned actions became ridiculous. By the decree of one county council, sauerkraut could be called only "liberty cabbage." Another local council renamed hamburger "liberty steak." A rabid teacher in Hilger wrote to the MCD that

> Last year we "weeded" out all german texts that were in our school library, clipped out all german songs in our books of national songs, blotted out the coat of arms and German flags in the dictionaries, and urged that every home destroy german text and library books they possess. We also spell germany without a capital letter. A few days ago we burned all of our *West's Ancient Worlds*, and I have the permission of our trustees to destroy any texts found to contain german propaganda.

This rampant patriotic hysteria spread throughout Montana society, to its very foundations. An incident at the Carpenter Creek School, seven miles southwest of Melstone, in Musselshell County, is illustrative. The *Roundup Record* reported,

> That Mrs. Hay, principal of the Carpenter Creek school, and Miss Vera Zinn, in charge of the primary room, have not been remiss in the teaching of patriotism was evidenced last Monday by an interesting occurrence in the schoolyard.

Shortly before the arrival of the teachers, a group of boys were discussing their rifle drill, when a new boy of Austrian parentage snatched a miniature flag from the cap of one of the primary pupils, made some disparaging remarks, and destroyed the flag.

In a few seconds, he was surrounded by boys of his own age who dispatched one of their number into the building for a large flag. Holding it out in front of the school house, they speedily compelled the young offender to kneel and kiss the folds of Old Glory.

Not satisfied with this demonstration of his change of heart, they escorted him into the school building and, before the assembled school, persuaded their captive to renew his act of allegiance before permitting him to seek the safety of his seat—a sadder and wiser boy.

Against this background of emotionalism, the Montana Legislature executed one of its two successful impeachments. On March 22, 1918, the Senate found Charles L. Crum, judge of the Fifteenth Judicial District, which included Rosebud and Musselshell Counties, guilty of "high crimes and misdemeanors and malfeasance in office." The removal of Judge Crum from the bench offers a strong lesson in the exercise of Constitutional rights.

Prior to his impeachment, Charles Liebert Crum's life exemplified dedication, commitment, success, and recognition. He was born on January 9, 1874, in Underwood, Indiana, to James W. and Sarah Houghland Crum. In 1884 the family moved to the Wilmot area of south-central Kansas. Charles ("C. L." to his family) attended nearby Winfield High School and spent two years at Southwestern College in Winfield. In 1894 Crum secured a job as the court reporter in the town of El Reno, Oklahoma Territory. Working diligently in his spare time, he read law with a local attorney until he successfully passed the Oklahoma bar exam and opened his own law practice.

Charles Crum married Jessie Helen Mitts of El Reno, a young woman of seventeen, in 1896. To the couple six children would be born, four of whom survived to adulthood. After the turn of the century, voters elected Crum a Canadian County judge, so he closed his law practice in El Reno. In 1902 he also filed on a sandhill homestead in Oklahoma, but quickly relinquished it when Jessie became ill. The family moved to Colorado temporarily, until her health improved somewhat.

C. L. learned in 1906 that the U.S. General Land Office had announced drawings for 160-acre farmland parcels within Montana's recent Crow Reservation cession. He immediately applied, since Montana's dry climate would be ideal for Jessie. Upon winning a chance to secure a bottomland farmstead in the Yellowstone Valley, Crum appeared at the Billings Land Office on August 6, 1906, and filed on the cash entry.

For the next few years, C. L. concentrated on raising his family and improving his homestead south of the Yellowstone River, between Hysham and Sanders. On November 1, 1906, the Crums moved into their new log home, and he subsequently constructed a 24 x 24 log barn, a 20 x 50 sheep shed, a corral, a root cellar, two wells, and more than two miles of wire fence. By 1908, when Crum received final patent for his homestead, he also had opened a storefront office in Sanders and had undertaken local legal work.

Although Jessie was only thirty years old at the time, her health deteriorated again with the birth of their last child, Frank, in 1909. As a result, C. L. relocated to Forsyth, the county seat of Rosebud County, and embarked on a full-time law practice. Crum's abilities quickly earned him a reputation as an efficient, diligent, and conscientious attorney. When he ran as a Republican for the position of Rosebud County Attorney in 1910, the *Forsyth Times-Journal* remarked, "He is not a grand-stander or a hot-air merchant, but a safe and conservative lawyer of the popular 'old school.'"

Voters elected Crum their county attorney by a wide margin (764 to 272) in 1910. In 1912 he ran on the Republican ticket for the four-year judgeship of Montana's Thirteenth Judicial District. In this election he defeated both an incumbent Democrat and a Progressive.

He assumed the bench in Forsyth in January 1913, at the age of thirty-nine.

Charles Crum's burdens had increased, however, during his rapid rise in the judiciary and in local popularity. In May 1910, Jessie had died at age 31, leaving the young attorney with five children to raise: Liebert, 13; Claude, 8; Maurice, 5; Dorothy, 3; Frank, 1. In typically methodical fashion, though, he hired a full-time housekeeper and arranged to spend as much time with his children as his duties would allow.

The reputation that Judge Crum built during this first term proved stellar. When the judge ran for reelection in 1916, he ran unopposed. The *Times-Journal* explained,

> There is no man on the bench in the State of Montana that has attained a more enviable record in the few short years that he has been there than has the Honorable Charles L. Crum. . . . There is no judge on the bench today that is held in higher esteem than is Judge Crum by the members of the bar who have had occasion to transact legal business before his court.
>
> Knowing the high standing of this man, those who would have otherwise aspired to this office have sidetracked the job this fall and are all lined up behind Judge Crum to a man.
>
> While he has no opposition in the field, he is appreciative of the good will of the people toward him and will, in the future as he has in the past, administer justice fairly and impartially to everybody.

By 1917, as the judge assumed the bench to begin his second term, his life had regained some normality. He had become a demonstrable success in his profession, and he had found Liebert a job in Costa Rica, working on ships bound through the Panama Canal. Claude had been somewhat sickly, but their new housekeeper—an Englishwoman by the name of Maude Battersby—had brought cohesion, discipline, and routine to the family.

Still, the European war consumed more and more of C. L.'s attention—particularly the Constitutional issues involved in neutrality
and in the proposed draft. Like millions of Americans of German
ancestry, Crum regretted seeing the United States wage war against
his ancestral fatherland, whatever the justifications. Perhaps the judge's
greatest weakness became his openness in discussing such matters
with his neighbors. In the end, this weakness encouraged his impeachment and precipitated his ruin.

Charles Liebert Crum's grandchildren agree that "even in discussing the weather, the Judge didn't speak, he orated. . . . Most of what
he said was delivered pompously, deliberately, . . . in capital letters."
As the 1917 war hysteria spread through Montana, that bombastic
characteristic began to aggravate acquaintances whom C. L. lectured
on America's bankrolling of the Allies, on U.S. entry into the war,
and on whether the Constitution permitted sending draftees
overseas.

Most of these neighbors excused C. L.'s loud, nonconformist views
on the war out of respect for the judge's office and for his solid, decade-long reputation in southeastern Montana. As the Presbyterian
minister in Forsyth noted, "[We] just threw the statements away with
the remark that 'He has gone crazy on the subject,' . . . that he talked
himself into a state of mind on it where he simply could not help but
talk about that." In addition to the war issues and the stress of working long hours and traveling to hold court outside Forsyth, C. L.
became increasingly worried about Claude's recurring illnesses.

Local dissatisfaction with Judge Crum's outspoken opposition to
the war coalesced after the United States declared war on Germany in
1917. In September of that year, the judge freed three reputed
members of the radical Industrial Workers of the World (IWW) from
the Rosebud County Jail. Although County Attorney Felkner F.
Haynes had obtained no evidence of their alleged arsonist activities,
he "knew these fellows to be bad actors." The three had been confined for days on bread and water before Judge Crum released them.

Shortly thereafter, a citizen approached C. L. at the Rosebud County Fair and asked him if the rumor were true that he would be removed from office because of this "pro-German action." Judge Crum reacted with vehemence to this allegation. Over the weekend he prepared a personal statement, which he read in open court prior to the resumption of a trial on Monday morning. He said, in part,

> Gentlemen, as American citizens, we owe no allegiance to any nation, to any government, or to any flag on earth except the American government and the American flag. Our rights, gentlemen, are defined by the Constitution of the United States. Among these rights is free speech. Of course, we differ. We always have, and we always will differ as to the policy to be adopted and pursued by this government. . . .
>
> While I recognize that the right of free speech justly and rightly has its limitation, any man—whether he be a public official or a private citizen, whether he be a man of wealth and power and influence or a poor man following the humble walks of life—who would deny his fellow man any other rights guaranteed by the Constitution fails to comprehend the object and purpose for which this government was established.
>
> Personally, gentlemen, I am absolutely now, and always have been, strictly pro-American. . . . I couldn't be anything else but pro-American if I wanted to—and I have no desire to be anything else. . . . Every dollar I have got on earth, even my life, is behind the American government. . . .
>
> Permit me to say in conclusion that I assume we are all loyal, patriotic American citizens. Let us do nothing that would make us unworthy of that proud distinction. Gentlemen, I thank you. (Applause).

C. L.'s public statement could not deflect the convictions of super-patriots who branded him a German sympathizer—and who saw in the passion of the times some opportunities for personal gain. In October 1917, Felkner Haynes—acting in a federal capacity—

investigated and arrested Rosebud County citizens Ves Hall and A. J. Just for sedition under the National Espionage Act. Haynes brought the two suspects to Forsyth. However, he did not jail them while he awaited instructions from U.S. District Attorney Burton K. Wheeler in Butte.

Hall and Just then consulted Judge Crum, who advised them to catch the next Northern Pacific passenger train for Butte to speak personally with Wheeler. The next morning, when Haynes discovered that the pair had departed Forsyth, he wired the Butte sheriff, who arrested and jailed the two men as they stepped from the train.

Although authorities filed federal indictments against both suspects, Felkner Haynes remained unsatisfied. In a statement released to the press, he fumed,

> It is time to go to the right or to the left! We must be either Americans or anti-Americans! There is no middle ground! . . . We prove ourselves allies of the Kaiser when we permit any person of whatever station in life to denounce the motives actuating the government in this struggle or to, in any way, sow the seeds of sedition.
>
> Our loyalty to the republic and to the soldiers and sailors is measured by the vigor with which we crush those who would disseminate the poison of disloyalty among us.

If anyone questioned that Haynes were attacking Judge Crum, he later testified,

> I felt that it was time for somebody to start the ball rolling down there with this fellow, so I published an interview in the press in eastern Montana, in which I told the people that he was a pro-German . . . that he was disseminating this German poison all through the country, that he was a disgrace to the bench, and that he ought to be removed.

Truly astute minds in Rosebud County recognized that such a bench vacancy logically could be filled by the incumbent county attorney.

The two attorneys from Forsyth faced off again when Federal Judge George M. Bourquin heard the Ves Hall case in Helena in January 1918. Haynes had compiled most of the evidence used to prosecute Hall; Crum appeared at the trial as a character witness for the defendant. Judge Bourquin—who, like U.S. Attorney Wheeler, maintained one of the saner heads during this period of surreal patriotism—listened to the evidence and, granting a defense motion for a directed verdict, acquitted Hall.

Following the trial, Haynes confronted Crum in the State Capitol hallway outside the attorney general's office. Judge Crum recounted,

> I started to leave the office, when I encountered Mr. Haynes. . . . He became very angry and stated that there would be a killing in Rosebud County within a very short time over the Hall decision. At the same time he rose from his seat and advanced toward me, telling me that I was pro-German.
>
> When I saw that I was about to be assaulted, I took my small automatic from my overcoat pocket and told him to stop. I also told him that he was an infamous liar, a thief, a perjurer, and I used many other vile names. The only thing that I am sorry for is that I have since learned that there was a young woman in an adjoining room who may have overhead my language.

Haynes's account of the showdown varies somewhat in detail, but neither man preferred charges as a result of the incident.

Next, Judge Crum's neighbors attacked him. As in some other Montana towns, the citizens of Forsyth had created a patriotic watchdog group—"the Committee of One Hundred"—to establish local standards of Americanism and to identify and intimidate "slackers." Although wholly extralegal, this *ad hoc* body carried the endorsement of the Rosebud County Council of Defense—indeed, several of the Council's executives doubled as leaders of "the Committee."

Two local attorneys, one of whom was Felkner Haynes, called a meeting of "the Committee" on February 2. After some heated discussion, the group brought in Judge Crum. The accusers instructed him to defend himself against charges ranging from his "non-participation in the war movements of the community" to the belief that he had advised his son Liebert to leave the country to avoid military conscription. The *Times-Journal* reported:

> At the close of the hearing, which lasted nearly two hours, Judge Crum retired. By a vote of those participating in the meeting, it was decided that the explanations offered by Judge Crum were not satisfactory, that he was not in sympathy with his constituency, and that his resignation should be asked for.
>
> A resolution was then offered directing that the chairman appoint a committee to wait upon the judge and to inform him that it was the desire of the meeting that he resign from the bench.

More than a week passed, however, before the committee could deliver its demand, as Judge Crum rushed off to the Miles City hospital, where his son Claude had fallen critically ill with cancer. For the next six weeks, C. L. would attempt to meet his court schedule in Roundup and Forsyth while spending every free minute at Claude's bedside—frequently sleeping in a chair in the hospital room. This routine would extract a real toll on his health, at the same time the community pressure on him increased.

When finally faced with the delegates from "the Committee of One Hundred," Crum refused to resign his judgeship. He found strength in a spontaneous meeting of more than eighty-five citizens in Roundup who drafted a supporting resolution. It stated, in part:

> Charles L. Crum has presided as Judge of the District Court in Musselshell County, Montana, for a period of six years, and . . . he is known generally to all the citizens in Roundup and Musselshell County

as an honest, honorable, and upright man and an able lawyer, a fair and impartial, fearless and conscientious Judge, impervious to personal and political influence. His personal and judicial record during his official career is above reproach and suspicion. . . .

But circumstances then presented Crum's enemies with another possibility. Governor Stewart had called a special session of the Fifteenth Legislature to address problems on the home front, such as the legalization of the Montana Council of Defense, the floating of seed-grain loans, and the passage of a strong sedition law. The special session sat in Helena from February 14 to February 25, 1918.

On February 21, Felkner Haynes delivered to Governor Stewart fifteen affidavits alleging Judge Crum's pro-German statements and actions. The governor immediately forwarded these documents to the House leadership, which generated Articles of Impeachment on the last day of the session. Felkner Haynes then resigned his position as Rosebud County Attorney, enlisted in the Army, and reported to Fort Wright, Washington. Officers served the Articles on Crum at his son's bedside in the Miles City hospital on February 28, 1918.

At this point, the pressure mounting against C. L. Crum seemed unbearable. Claude clearly was dying of cancer; many of his neighbors in Forsyth had joined the vigilante "Committee of One Hundred" to remove him from office; the Senate had scheduled his impeachment trial for March 20. The judge suffered a nervous breakdown during the first week of March, and his physician confined him to bed in Miles City.

Three noted Montana attorneys volunteered their services in Crum's defense—Judge O. H. Fletcher Goddard of Billings, and Sharpless Walker and Judge Charles H. Loud of Miles City. Judge Crum's defense team faced problems, however, not the least of which involved his weakened condition. This distinguished team outlined its defense, conferred with colleagues across the state about the mood of the Senate and the people, and brought its findings to C. L. They persuaded the judge that his resignation offered the most expedient solution, the best one for his health—*if* such a resignation would kill the impeachment proceedings.

After receiving a promise from Governor Stewart that he would recommend suspending the Senate trial, Fletcher Goddard carried Judge Crum's dictated resignation to Helena. The governor received the resignation on March 10, 1918. It stated,

> This action on my part is not a confession that I have been guilty of any crime. In fact, I have violated no law and have not been guilty of any malfeasance or misfeasance in office. Neither does it mean that I am afraid to face any charges which have been made against me. I have never been accused of being either a coward or a quitter.
>
> My action simply means that there is a limit to human endurance and that I have reached that limit. . . .
>
> It may be possible that I have made some careless and reckless statements or criticisms of the policy adopted and followed by the present National Administration, but I have never meant or intended at any time to be in the least disloyal to the American Government. . . .

Despite Crum's tendered resignation and an apparent agreement that the impeachment would be nullified, Governor Stewart submitted the document to the House managers without recommendation. Although the goal of deposing Judge Crum from the bench had been accomplished, the House decided to proceed with the impeachment— because "a conviction would exert a wholesome effect in stamping out German propagandists."

In the meantime, however, C. L. believed that his resignation had terminated the move to impeach him. Since Claude's condition had improved temporarily, the judge—on the advice of his physician— returned to Forsyth, packed a bag, and departed Montana (March 10) to escape the harassment that he had endured for months. In all probability, he traveled to visit family members in Kansas and Oklahoma.

The impeachment trial of Judge Charles L. Crum opened in the Montana Senate on March 20, 1918, orchestrated by the Board of House Managers. In his letter of resignation, C. L. had noted:

> I also feel that a trial of my case would simply provide an opportunity for certain people to pose before the public and in the press as super-patriots. It would give these people an opportunity to color and distort statements I have made until they have no resemblance to the true facts. It would enable some of my bitter personal enemies to continue to spread their venom and poison and pollute the atmosphere. It would inflame the public mind and cost the State of Montana many thousands of dollars. . . .

The judge could not have characterized the three-day proceedings more aptly! Not only was Crum absent and unable to defend himself, but also no legal counsel appeared in his behalf. Early in the trial, Senator Fred Whiteside of Kalispell noted this inequity. (Many Montanans already respected Whiteside for his exposure of corruption in the First Capitol Commission and in W. A. Clark's attempt to gain a U.S. Senate seat by bribing members of the Legislature.) He proposed that the Senate appoint someone to examine witnesses in Crum's behalf, arguing,

> I think that there ought to be someone to represent that side of the case. Otherwise a proceeding of this kind is merely a farce. It is trying dead issues here. Judge Crum has already been convicted by public opinion. He will never hold office in this State again, whether he is convicted of this or not. . . . But if this proceeding is to go on, I think that the other side should be represented.

Whiteside's motion failed on a voice vote.

What followed proved a charade, a litany of hearsay and circumstantial evidence interspersed with posturing by the interrogating

House managers and by some vehement senators. Denouncers declared that Judge Crum had criticized the President, the Congress, and the British while reveling in German victories—particularly the sinking of the *Lusitania*. Witnesses testified that they heard Crum both oppose U.S. entry into the war and question the Constitutionality of national conscription. They asserted that the judge voiced these statements both before and after the U.S. had declared war on Germany, and that he had brought dishonor on his office. Witnesses repeatedly cited Crum's defense of the civil liberties of IWW members as "disloyal" and "un-American."

At one point in the trial, Senator Whiteside characterized the nature of the prosecution's case, saying, "Certainly ninety per cent of the testimony that has been introduced here has been hearsay and irrelevant testimony." Nevertheless, when the final vote occurred on March 22, senators found Charles L. Crum guilty of all six Articles of Impeachment. The resultant Senate Resolution concluded:

[We] do find the said Charles L. Crum guilty of high crimes, misdemeanors, and malfeasance in office as charged. . . . And do hereby order and adjudge that he be removed from the office of the Judge of the District Court. . . . and that he be disqualified to hold any office of honor, trust, or profit under the State of Montana.

Of the verdict, Burton K. Wheeler reflected, "I considered this a tragedy, for I thought Crum a fine and honorable man."

With the witch-hunt concluded, Montana newspapers such as the *Helena Independent*, which consistently fueled war hysteria, claimed a monumental victory for America and Americanism. In fact, the impeachment of Judge Crum *did* serve a definite purpose: coupled with the extreme Montana Sedition Act passed by the Extraordinary Session in February 1918, the conviction of Crum alerted all Montanans that the principle of free speech would be suspended in this state until further notice.

Charles Liebert Crum never did recover from the devastation of his impeachment. The balance of his life—almost thirty years—constituted a long, slow slide into bitterness and alcoholism. Only one month after the Senate trial, Claude Crum died of cancer at the family home in Forsyth. C. L. returned to bury his sixteen-year-old son next to his wife, then again left Montana. His family believes that he spent the balance of 1918 in Mexico City, perhaps in the company of Liebert. World War I ended on November 11, 1918.

Crum returned to Forsyth in January 1919, to join his housekeeper, Maude Battersby, and his family: Maurice, 14; Dorothy, 12; and Frank, 9. The *Forsyth Democrat*, sympathetic to Crum's plight, published a postwar interview with the judge in which he indicated that he had "learned his lesson:"

> There remain questions about the war which I cannot discuss. Someone, it matters not whom, might differ from my views. . . . Then what show would a man have against a charge of disloyalty, no matter how false, slanderous, or malicious it might be? . . . Of course, under such conditions, I can only remain silent.

To forestall any feelings of guilt or sympathy that might be engendered in the community, the rival *Forsyth Times-Journal* countered with a vitriolic editorial that played all the patriotic cards. After ridiculing Crum's perspective, the writer concluded that Forsyth could not forgive the fallen man. Evidently C. L. agreed, since he quietly relocated his housekeeper and his children in Center, North Dakota, just northwest of Bismarck, in August 1919.

In Center, the experienced attorney rapidly developed a local clientele and frequently worked as the deputy Oliver County attorney. Liebert rejoined the family and became principal of the Center Public School. The younger children excelled in grade-school activities. In the spring of 1920, the local chapter of the Non-Partisan League (NPL)—a leftist agrarian political party of real strength in the state—nominated C. L. for county attorney. He subsequently relinquished that nomination to become the NPL's candidate for the State House from Oliver County in the July 1920 primary.

However, the specter of C. L.'s Montana impeachment again loomed to quash his aspirations. Members of Center's American Legion post contacted the editor of the Forsyth *Times-Journal,* who provided newspaper clippings and a copy of the Montana Senate's impeachment proceedings. Still riding a national wave of super-patriotism, the Legion devoted its June 1920 issue of the *Inland Post* magazine to a detailed review of the charges leveled against Judge Crum in the Montana Senate trial. When they also discovered that C. L. did not meet the residency requirement for the House seat, he withdrew from the ticket. Attorney Crum moved his law practice and his family to Mandan that September.

Quietly Charles L. Crum tried to reconstruct his life by building an active legal practice in Bismarck–Mandan during the 1920s. After Liebert graduated from the University of North Dakota Law School in 1924, he joined his father in the firm and enjoyed some statewide political success during the 1930s. However, the judge's spirit had been broken. His dedication to law dissipated, and his practice be-came pedestrian, predictable. When C. L. retired just before World War II, he had become a disillusioned man who increasingly found solace in drink.

During the war, C. L. moved to California to live with Liebert and his family. When Liebert died in 1945, however, the judge returned to Kansas to join his sister, Ada Crum Akers, on a farm just outside of Wilmot. There he died of diabetes on March 21, 1948; family mem-bers buried him in the Wilmot Cemetery. His obituary in the local newspaper ran less than four column inches and never mentioned the 1918 impeachment that ruined his life. Montana newspapers ig-nored his death completely.

In his 1919 interview in the *Forsyth Democrat,* the judge had remarked:

I feel that time and transpiring events will more clearly vindicate my post than anything I could say or do. I have a sublime faith in the natural honesty and sense of justice of the American people. I feel sure that, at some future time, the right-thinking people of the State of Montana will undo the wrong that has been inflicted upon me.

The judgment against Charles Crum *would be* set aside by resolution of the Montana Senate—more than seventy years after the impeachment of a man whose greatest crimes comprised his belief in the democratic principal of free speech and his delivery of nonconformist opinions too openly, too loudly. In the absence of the patriotic hysteria that superheated Montana during the 1916-1921 period, the people of Montana would clear the name of Charles Liebert Crum.

In 1990, after seeing this essay in *Montana Magazine, Great Falls Tribune* reporter Steve Shirley wrote a persuasive column summarizing the Crum impeachment. In Montana's Fifty-Second Legislature, Senator Harry Fritz of Missoula and nine cosponsors subsequently introduced *Senate Resolution #2*, to exonerate Judge Crum from the wrongful impeachment of March 22, 1918. Hearings before the Senate Judiciary Committee on January 25, 1991, resulted in a unanimous "do pass" recommendation, and the resolution moved quickly to the full Senate.

On January 26, 1991, the Montana Senate voted 46-0 in favor of Senate Resolution #2. Visitors in the gallery to witness this precedent-setting action included the judge's grandchildren—Darwin R. Crum of Schaumburg, Illinois, and Patricia Crum Scott of Pleasanton, California. Following their vote, in an emotional scene, the senators stood and applauded the Crum descendants long and loud. After almost seventy-three years, the judge's unjust burden of dishonor had been lifted.

CHAPTER 12

THE RONAN STATE BANK
ROBBERY, 1929

At noon on June 18, 1929, two masked men robbed the Ronan State Bank and escaped in a green Hudson touring car. They stole $3,000—half of which pack rats ate before it could be spent. They injured two bank employees, although both recovered. Officers fairly quickly captured the robbers, as well as their drivers. Montana authorities incarcerated the stick-up artists at the State Penitentiary in Deer Lodge that November. This would appear to be a simple story, demonstrating once again that "crime does not pay"—a tale hardly remarkable enough to report.

However, the story of the Ronan State Bank robbery is more complicated than that. It overlays at least five other crimes. It becomes a story of many "jobs," of a gang of self-styled toughs, of fast, sleek touring cars, of a speedy but easily manipulated justice system, and of clear stereotypes. Moreover it offers entertainment—lurid newspaper stories that appeared long before television brought us *Dragnet, Charlie's Angels, Hill Street Blues, Miami Vice,* or *NYPD Blue.* The Ronan State Bank robbery remains indelibly a story just of those times, just of that year, in Montana.

In the American chronology, the year 1929 is most memorable. Herbert Hoover had just been elected President. Montana's Prohibition was eleven years old; national Prohibition was ten, and only four years short of repeal. The 1920s had spawned jazz, a new kind of cynicism about work, the weakening of long-held taboos, motion picture "talkies," uneven economic fortunes, Charles Lindbergh's transatlantic flight, and collective self-indulgence. By 1929 one in every five Americans owned an automobile; "machines" had evolved from oddities to necessities to status symbols.

Historians either credit Prohibition with creating a decade of concerted hypocrisy, or treat it as the by-product of a new national naughtiness. Either way, Prohibition produced gangsters—some of whom gained fame as "social bandits." In their romanticized lawlessness, these gangsters marketed liquor and other illegal pleasures. They often got away with criminal activity. On St. Valentine's Day in 1929, for instance, Chicago mobster Al Capone's men killed seven members of a rival gang—and still he could not be convicted of the crime. Then, on "Black Tuesday," October 29, 1929, the New York Stock Exchange crashed. Finally the whole country knew what Montana farmers and ranchers had been saying throughout the 1920s: "Tough times are *here!*" The Ronan State Bank robbery and its related crimes fit neatly into the final months of the 1920s, epitomizing the times.

The story of the robbery began in mid-June 1929. In a practice unusual for its day, the Ronan State Bank remained open through the noon hour to accommodate working people and farmers. On Tuesday, June 18, head cashier Harold Olsson and assistant cashier Vernon Hollingsworth had remained on duty and saw two masked men enter the empty bank lobby, waving pistols. The thieves predictably shouted "Stick 'em up!" and told the cashiers to "Hit the floor!" Although the two men started to comply, the robbers knocked both Olsson and Hollingsworth insensible.

One bandit stood guard while the other entered the vault and tried to open the safe. Failing this task—and under pressure as bank customers began to arrive—the robbers gathered only loose money from the cash drawers and a stack of wrapped coins before rushing from the building.

THE MARTIN-GROTE GANG
JUNE-NOVEMBER, 1929

Unpaved Surface
Paved Surface

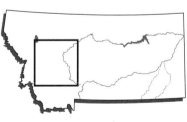

Although dazed and bleeding, Olsson and Hollingsworth responded quickly. The latter grabbed the bank's revolver, ran outside, spotted the green Hudson getaway car, and fired into the air to alert townspeople. Olsson comforted several frightened customers and dashed out in time to see Hollingsworth running after the Hudson, firing his gun, then falling in the dirt—shot in the arm by the thieves.

Word of the robbery spread rapidly. Lake County Sheriff W. H. Needham immediately recruited a local attorney and a tribal policeman to chase the Hudson north on Highway 93. He telephoned Polson to warn city officials that their banks might be next. A highway worker near Pablo told Needham that he had seen the Hudson running north on the graveled highway and had watched two men jump out and dash into the timber while a third man drove the auto farther north. Then the trail cooled. The robbers seemed to have vanished.

The Burns Detective Agency, hired by the American Banking Association, directly sent its representative from Spokane. Yet only when a local rancher spotted the abandoned green Hudson in the woods near Pablo could Needham proceed. At the site of the auto, the sheriff found multiple clues: tire tracks from a second getaway car; the remains of a campfire; a burned cap with the name "Ganny" inside it; a matchbook; pieces of hotel stationery with a hand-written address on one of them; a pair of coveralls; a dropped roll of bills.

From this evidence, Needham linked the matchbook to Helena's "The Mint"—a saloon converted into a cigar store by Prohibition—and the stationery to Helena's Placer Hotel. He discovered that "Ganny" referred to Ganny Boone, whose family lived at the Helena address scrawled on the stationery. Ganny proved a reliable character, but he had a ne'er-do-well brother, Easton, whose arrest record for fighting and Prohibition violations suggested his involvement.

Needham concluded that four or five men had conducted the bank heist. He believed they had used a second getaway car to escape south on Highway 93, running right through the heart of Ronan, while lawmen tried to get organized. By June 20, the *Ronan Pioneer* asserted, "The robbery is, without doubt, the work of an expert gang and was carefully planned out. . . . No effort is being spared to bring about the gang's capture."

Once linked with Lewis and Clark County Sheriff Clyde Burgess, Sheriff Needham traveled to Helena and there arrested Easton Boone on June 23. By July 27, authorities had bound Boone over to district court in Polson. He fit the description that Olsson and Hollingsworth offered for one robber, and evidence specifically implicating Boone impressed the Polson judge. No counsel represented Boone, and he could post no bond. He neither confessed to the crime nor implicated anyone.

Still, newspapers repeated Needham's initial belief that the robbery involved four or five men—"an expert gang"—and at least two cars. For another couple of weeks, without any particular evidence, the press speculated that lawmen were investigating various gang members. Notwithstanding the newspaper melodrama, Sheriff Needham's initial belief proved absolutely correct. By September, Needham and law-enforcement officers in Helena, Anaconda, Great Falls, Boulder, Missoula, and St. Ignatius could show that the Ronan bank job had been committed by four men—all members of a seven-member gang.

Easton Boone and Martin Jensen were indeed the two masked men who had robbed the Ronan bank on June 18. Martin Ernst and Joe Brennan had served as their drivers. All four men were in their twenties, with shady reputations and small-time records. The gang also included Tom Martin, Floyd Grote, and Robert Bowers. Martin was an older, savvy criminal who sported a long record of serious crimes throughout the West. Joe Brennan's wife, Mary, and a Helena floozy named Bobby Kelly often ran with these characters.

The story of how Montana lawmen investigated and captured the bank-robbery gang enlivened the front pages of Montana newspapers though the summer of 1929. Each development in this drama left the statewide audience begging for the next episode. The saga includes several key incidents:

On July 14, 1929, unidentified robbers hit the Green Mill (Lantern) Dance Hall near Great Falls and escaped with about a thousand dollars. Authorities drew no immediate connection between this holdup and the Ronan bank job, however. Instead, they followed other leads. That same Sunday evening, Sheriff Needham drove to Helena the green Hudson recovered in the woods near Pablo. He planned to deliver the auto to an insurance-company representative, who would return it to its rightful owner in Gillette, Wyoming. Needham parked the distinctive car in front of the Lewis and Clark County jail and registered at a local hotel.

Shortly after one o'clock on Monday morning, "persons unknown" set the Hudson afire. The (Polson) *Flathead Courier* speculated:

> The officials planted the car and lay in wait to see who came. They did not expect it to be burned, however, but hoped an attempt would be made to steal it. Needham is not saying anything; the Burns [Detective Agency] men lie low. But the story will not disappear that hidden sleuths saw who fired the car and took the new trails in consequence.

On July 16, two days later, Sheriff Needham captured the second Ronan robber, Martin Ernst, in Anaconda. Needham had tracked Ernst with the help of witnesses who spotted an unfamiliar, big Buick in the Ronan vicinity just before the robbery. Ernst reportedly had driven the stolen Buick to a Fourth of July celebration in Lincoln, then all around Helena, and finally to Anaconda, where he sought work. Although Ernst dictated no statement after his capture, Montana newspapers surmised that lawmen tentatively had identified other Ronan bandits and that the search focused on Helena.

On July 23, "thugs" brandishing automatic pistols robbed and severely beat the ticket agent and a waiting passenger at the elegant Great Northern Depot in Helena. Several witnesses watched the robbers depart the depot, climb into their automobile, and race west out of town. These informants argued, however, over whether the machine was a green touring car or a green sedan. Other witnesses had seen side curtains and different front and rear license plates on the auto.

That night, on the Helena-Great Falls road, highwaymen in two cars (a coupe and a sedan) stopped, beat, and robbed three Butte travelers. A bit later, several thieves held up a filling station in Wolf Creek. Authorities later learned that the coupe had been a Studebaker stolen from the Chevalier Ranch north of Helena.

On the next afternoon—based on automobile and license-tag descriptions and on an anonymous telephone call—Cascade and Lewis and Clark County sheriffs and their deputies ambushed a shack on the Missouri River southwest of Great Falls. With a volley of shots, they flushed from the cabin two men who surrendered: Martin Jensen and Robert Bowers. Two other occupants, Tom Martin and Floyd Grote, dashed into the trees and escaped. This pair deliberately had sacrificed the gang's youngest members for their own freedom.

With the capture of Jensen and Bowers, officers received a huge break: Jensen talked. He admitted his role in the Green Mill Dance Hall holdup and in the Great Northern Depot heist. He also fingered Tom Martin and Floyd Grote as the brains of the operation. Jensen's statement corroborated a photo of Tom Martin identified by the Great Northern ticket agent. Bowers did not talk, but the Montana press immediately (and incorrectly) linked him to the Ronan robbery.

Just over a week later, Jensen and Bowers pled guilty to the Green Mill Dance Hall holdup, and each received a term of twenty years in the Montana State Penitentiary. Neither young man confessed to more than standing guard at the Great Northern Depot job. Both admitted, however, that Martin had lured them into similar ventures with the promise of "easy money." Newspapers reported that the "green getaway machine" had been a green Marquette sedan stolen in Sandpoint, Idaho.

Suddenly the focus of all activity shifted west. Easton Boone's trial for the Ronan State Bank robbery began on August 19 in Polson, with Helena attorney Lester Loble defending him. Martin Ernst's trial would follow immediately in the Lake County seat. Then, shortly after midnight on August 20—just down the road from Polson at St. Ignatius—three bandits awoke Mission State Bank cashier A. P. Morse and his family in their beds. Two criminals drove Morse to his bank at gunpoint and demanded that he open the safe. The Mission State Bank recently had installed an electric timer on its safe, however, so the thwarted trio forced Morse to carry the bank's loose silver to his home, gathered up his wife and two children, Verna and Buddy, and pushed them into getaway cars.

The thieves drove south in the Morses' brand-new Nash and in a green Oakland coach. On Evaro Hill, when the Nash ran out of gasoline, the bandits punctured its tires, abandoned the family, and headed toward Missoula in the Oakland. Morse reported that only one gunman had worn a mask and that another, apparently the leader, was talkative and drunk—sipping moonshine during much of the escapade. Two days later, Lewis and Clark County Sheriff Burgess began receiving reports that the Oakland coach had been seen in Helena, then in Boulder, and then Meaderville, near Butte. A clerk in a Boulder soft-drink parlor tentatively identified the suspects as Joe Brennan, Tom Martin, and another person, probably a woman.

Then, on the night of August 21, Butte businessman James Thomas stopped his auto on the way home from Anaconda to help a stranded female motorist—"a woman dressed all in white." Two men quickly appeared from the shadows, bound and gagged Thomas, and stole his Hudson. Before departing, they pushed the green Oakland coach used in the St. Ignatius robbery into the barrow pit and set it afire. The next day, the Montana Bankers Association called attention to its $2,000 reward, offered to the person who could produce "any dead bank robbers."

Meanwhile back in Polson, as the trials of Boone and Ernst proceeded late in August, all hell broke loose! Thirty of the defendants'

friends—in Polson ostensibly to vouch for the pair's good character—terrorized the area, carrying weapons and threatening local citizens. Mrs. Olsson, wife of the Ronan bank cashier, answered her front
door to find three intimidating outsiders asking for her husband. A
local dairy quit delivering in the evening after being threatened by
unknown toughs. Polson residents reported large, dark cars cruising
through their neighborhoods and strangers inquiring about banks
and banking officials.

In response, Sheriff Needham deputized every reliable person he
could find. Judge Asa L. Duncan, on the bench at Boone's trial,
authorized state witnesses to arm themselves. Residents burned their
house lights all night, and merchants hired their own private guards
and stationed them in their businesses. Even with all these precau-
tions, unknown persons broke into and ransacked the home of Lake
County Attorney Grover Johnson, prosecutor of the Boone and Ernst
cases.

Boone's trial quickly became a battle of alibis. The defendant mus-
tered family and friends who placed him in several Helena locations
on June 18. Thus the Boone case ended in a hung jury, and the judge
freed Boone—just as he impaneled another jury for Ernst.

The Ernst trial developed differently. The prosecution presented
the testimony of Helena taxi driver Eugene Wenzler to counter the
defense's alibis. Early in July, a drunken Ernst had visited Wenzler's
cabin outside Helena with a back seat full of guns, bragging about his
prowess as a bank robber. Ernst boasted of supplying the guns and
some gasoline to Tom Martin, Floyd Grote, and Joe Brennan at a
nearby cabin.

While attorneys traded charges about which man in this pair was
too drunk to be credible, Wenzler's information obviously proved
pivotal because it tied both Ernst and Brennan to the Ronan bank
job. In summation, County Attorney Johnson swept aside the defense's
alibis and added, "Many men have robbed banks. But how much
more despicable it is to bring an aged father and mother into a court-

room and make them perjure themselves." The Polson jury quickly convicted Ernst, who spent the night preparing his full confession.

On August 31, lawmen—acting on a tip—ambushed whiskey-runner Tom Flavin's cabin south of Helena, in Jefferson County. Armed with sawed-off shotguns and repeating rifles, officers surrounded the shack while Sheriff Burgess coasted his police car down the slope above the cabin and shined a spotlight directly inside. After a few warning shots, Mary Brennan and Bobby Kelly appeared, dressed in coveralls, and surrendered. When no one else emerged, lawmen opened fire on the cabin. Tom Martin and Joe Brennan quickly shouted that they too would surrender. Authorities never did locate Floyd Grote, that autumn or later.

In perfunctory ten-minute proceedings in Polson on September 10, Easton Boone and Joe Brennan pled guilty to the Ronan State Bank stickup. They entered the State Prison on September 12, each carrying a fifteen-year sentence. Bobby Kelly—"the woman in white"—confessed to nothing. In fact, during September she waffled, first offering "to tell all" in exchange for immunity, then insisting on her innocence. The (Helena) *Record-Herald* described Kelly as

> unusually attractive . . . [although] her speech teems with the vernacular of the street. . . . Mrs. Kelly continued to keep up her chic appearance when she appeared for her hearing in Anaconda, clad in a Lindbergh helmet, black coat, sheer silk hose, and spike-heeled shoes.

In October, Kelly finally stood trial in Anaconda. She pled "not guilty" on all charges. Her attorney portrayed Bobby as a simple, innocent victim of circumstance—blinded by alcohol to the effects of her actions. Tom Martin testified in her defense that, in fact, he purposefully had kept her ignorant of all the plots. The jury acquitted "the woman in white" of all charges.

Officers tried Tom Martin, the real brains of the outfit, in Helena for the Great Northern Depot heist. Although Jensen attempted to recant his confession implicating Martin, prosecutors presented an eyewitness identification by the beaten railroad clerk. The jury deliberated only ten minutes before convicting Martin on November 7. Authorities immediately escorted him to Deer Lodge to begin a fifty-year prison term. Montana's 1929 summer crime spree had concluded.

This brief episode in Montana history provides more than just lurid reading. It produces more than just a glimpse of Montana's low-budget version of the Al Capone hoodlums or the bank robberies of Charles "Pretty Boy" Floyd. This cops-and-robbers story accurately reflects Montana in the late 1920s. For example, the only paved roads in the state were short stretches around Butte and Anaconda. Lawmen often used a combination of railroad and automobile travel to cover Montana, since all auto travel was seasonal. Also typical of the era, gang members brazenly drove stolen, flamboyant, touring cars— not inconspicuous Model-A Fords—in committing their crimes. Further, local lawmen welcomed trained-detective assistance from such companies as the Burns Detective Agency and the Great Northern Railway.

Justice in the 1920s seems swift by current standards. The system brought accused criminals to trial quickly, and a guilty verdict resulted in an immediate, stiff sentence and imprisonment. In this case, authorities concluded all legal action involving the seven gang members less than five months after the *beginning* of their crime spree. Interestingly, liquor figured prominently as an influencer of events in 1929. All parties assumed the presence of alcohol—despite eleven years of Montana Prohibition.

What the story of this 1929 gang of thieves best reveals is how susceptible the Montana public was to a continuing saga of outrageous crime—complete with fast cars, unnecessary violence, a mysterious "woman in white," and methodical, unrelenting lawmen. Montanans displayed a voracious appetite for every juicy tidbit fed to them by local newspapers.

Similar scenarios had played elsewhere in the nation during the 1920s, and they would run again across the country during the Depression. To Montanans—as to the rest of the American public—some of this scenario's attraction derived from widespread "hard times" and social malaise. The Montana version packed lots of drama; it also suffered an extremely short run.

CHAPTER 13

MONTANA'S WARTIME JAPANESE

On December 7, 1941, the Japanese Imperial Navy engineered an early morning surprise attack on the United States' Pearl Harbor naval base in Hawaii. During the two-hour assault, Japanese forces sank or disabled 19 ships, destroyed more than 150 U.S. planes, killed 2,335 soldiers and sailors, and wounded 1,178 military personnel. This dramatic raid thrust Montana—and the rest of the country—into a total, five-year war. "This day that will live in infamy" and World War II so changed the economic, demographic, and social configurations of the state that they mark a clear historical watershed. Never again could Montanans legitimately argue that they lived unaffected by national and international forces.

When Congress declared war on Japan on December 8, 1941, only Montana's Representative Jeannette Rankin voted "nay." Dismissing Rankin's peculiarity, Montanans immediately embarked on an emotional immersion in the war effort. Although state residents historically have been schizophrenic in trying to orient themselves beyond Montana borders, Montanans adopted a West Coast, Pacific-theater perception of the war. The rumored possibility of Japanese attacks on the Pacific coastline reinforced this view. The subsequent 1944-1945 fear of Japanese incendiary balloons—at least thirty-two of which landed in Montana—similarly fed a such a perspective.

The surprise attack on Pearl Harbor had quickly focused some Montanans' outrage on the duplicitous Japanese. Dormant anti-Oriental racism burst into Montana newspapers, expressed in such terms as "Nips," "Japs," and "Rising Suns." Political cartoons likewise featured crafty, inscrutable Japanese caricatures. Within one month, these newspapers were running U.S. government propaganda-machine portrayals of "Tojo—the Enemy." They admonished Montanans to "Kick the Japs in the Butt" by buying war bonds, conserving resources, and increasing farm, forest, and mine production.

The 1940 federal census for Montana listed only 508 persons of Japanese ancestry in Montana. Forty-five percent of these people were *Issei*, or immigrants born in Japan. Many of the *Issei* worked for the Milwaukee Road, Great Northern, or Northern Pacific railroads. They concentrated in such railroad towns as Miles City, Livingston, Deer Lodge, Missoula, and Havre. Because of the National Immigration Act of 1924, the federal government considered most of these *Issei* "aliens ineligible to citizenship."

However, fifty-five percent of the Montana Japanese were *Nisei*, or American-born persons of Japanese ancestry—that is, citizens of the United States. They resided in communities all across the state, often employed as merchants, professionals, service-sector workers, and farmers.

Because the Japanese comprised less than one-thousandth of the Montana population, and because they maintained a low social profile, prewar Montanans had tended to assess the Japanese among them as individuals. That perception changed dramatically with the attack on Pearl Harbor. In the irrational xenophobia that swept the nation following the attack, no person of Japanese ancestry remained truly safe. Fear, confusion, anger, and the need to retaliate inspired distrust for, and hatred of, *all Japanese*.

On the night of December 7, a Missoula County deputy sheriff drove to Superior. Here he took into protective custody six Japanese-American Northern Pacific crewmen who had been threatened with

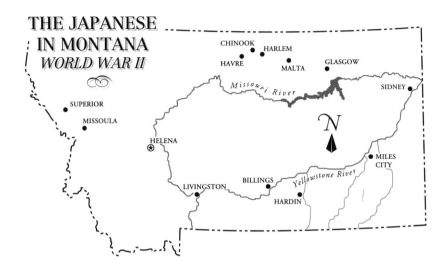

THE JAPANESE
IN MONTANA
WORLD WAR II

lynching by a mob of white townspeople. The lawman spirited the train workers up the mainline to spend two nights in the Missoula County jail. Authorities then sent the men, under protective guard, to their homes in Livingston.

On the morning of December 8, white railroadmen in the Milwaukee Road shops in Miles City refused to begin their shift until company officials removed seven of their Japanese-American coworkers. The Custer County sheriff escorted these Japanese men back to their homes, and work began.

In Havre, on December 8, Sheriff R. C. Timmons declared the need for citizens' vigilance to witness and report conversations involving suspected espionage and sabotage:

> Anyone who hears a conversation or observes an act which seems suspicious should report the matter at once to a competent enforcement officer. In reporting any such matters, the one making the report should be sure to be able to tell where it took place and when, what was said or done, and who else heard it said or saw it done.

The sheriff further promised the anonymity and the protection of any informer. In a community on the high plains—some 750 air miles from the Pacific Ocean—which included an identifiable Japanese-American population, (Havre) *Daily News* readers never questioned who was the subject of this citizen-surveillance program.

In Chinook, Chief of Police Herb Friede and Blaine County Sheriff C. B. Reser notified all "enemy aliens" that they must deposit their cameras and short-wave radio sets at the sheriff's office within three days, announcing, "The failure to surrender these articles will result in their forfeiture and in the arrest of the alien-enemy owner for internment in an Army detention camp for the duration of the war."

Some state and community officials, and some private Montanans, were able to maintain their sense of justice. These few continued to differentiate between Japanese-Americans—the holders of Constitutionally-guaranteed civil rights—and the Japanese military leaders who were directing the Pacific-theater offensive. However, this rational minority proved virtually powerless in the face of a super-patriotic public sentiment that condemned all persons of Japanese ancestry.

State Defense Coordinator Tom Caverly asked all sheriff's officers to warn the Japanese-Americans in their counties that remaining quietly in their homes offered the best protection from their fellow Montanans. In Butte, William Hong, president of the Butte Korean Club, recognized that many Montanans could not, or would not, distinguish Koreans from Japanese. To protect themselves, members of the organization wore badges and placed stickers on their automobiles and house windows that declared, "I Am A Korean."

In the months following the Pearl Harbor attack, Montanans redirected their activities to support the national war effort. The state fought the Axis powers primarily in two ways. First, it provided young men and women for military service, through enlistment and the national draft. Second, on the home front, its residents subscribed to war bond drives, conserved such precious materials as gasoline, rubber, and foodstuffs, and increased their industrial and agricultural production. Throughout, Montanans never lost sight of the Japanese enemy.

The state's two-pronged offensive proved successful. From a population of 559,456 in 1940, Montana furnished 57,000 persons for the military—or more than ten percent of its population. Thousands of other residents moved to the West Coast to work in war-material factories. In addition, Montana established a national record as the first state to oversubscribe to *eight* World War II savings-bond drives. Despite the reduction in its work force, Montana raised production levels in agriculture, forestry, mining, and transportation. Montanans committed themselves to an Allied victory with a vengeance.

During the early months of 1942, newspaper and radio reminders of their war involvement bombarded the state's residents. Registers ran in the newspapers of local youths enlisting in the service, of men designated by the county Selective Service Board, and of local subscribers to War Fund drives. Newspaper articles and radio broadcasts admonished Montanans to contribute to drives for scrap metal, brown paper, phonograph records, nylons, and lard. Those same media provided instructions on planting "Victory Gardens," on reconditioning machinery parts, and on using ration books, ration stamps, and ration tokens for everything from butter to lumber to meat to gasoline to sugar.

A constant news feature was the announcement of local boys missing-in-action, wounded, or killed—frequently at the hands of the Japanese war machine. Censored "letters to the editor" from local boys overseas regularly brought the crude realities of war into Montana sitting rooms and kitchens. The average Montanan was assailed daily with the propaganda concept that the Japanese were the godless, vicious, deceitful enemy.

Initially this concerted anti-Japanese sentiment erupted in Missoula, where the issue had been simmering for months. Well before the attack on Pearl Harbor, the Federal Bureau of Investigation

(FBI) had developed a "suspect list of potentially dangerous enemy aliens." It established two locations for alien internment camps—should they ever be needed. One of the sites was in Bismarck, North Dakota; the other was in Missoula, Montana. By April 1941, the U.S. Army had transferred jurisdiction of its Fort Missoula complex to the Immigration and Naturalization Service (INS). The head of the U.S. Justice Department's Alien Enemy Control Unit became the supervisor of the two camps.

Shortly after the December 7 attack, the FBI arrested Germans, Italians, and Japanese on its "alien suspect list" and transported them to either Bismarck or Missoula. Most internees at Fort Missoula were of Italian and Japanese extraction, with Japanese suspects predominant. Within days, rumors of imminent danger swept the Missoula community. The reality of World War II had reached Montana, quickly and graphically.

The depth of many Missoula residents' opposition to Japanese-Americans is revealed in a letter from one of the city's leading attorneys, Howard Toole, to Montana Governor Sam C. Ford in April 1942. The letter was written in response to a suggestion made by Dr. Ernest O. Melby, president of Montana State University (now The University of Montana), who had stated publicly that he would be receptive to enrolling in the Missoula school Japanese-American students evacuated from the University of Washington. Toole wrote,

> Dear Governor:
> I called you by phone yesterday because I was anxious to stop any possible reaction which might occur in this community from Dr. Melby's suggestion that Japanese students might be acceptable at the University. This community, as you know, has just gone through considerable discussion, with substantial opposition, to bringing in Japanese labor. . . .
>
> Dr. Melby's statement came out in the morning *Missoulian*, on the same day when the Missoula County draft numbers were announced.

... One woman, whose son has a low draft number and is a junior at the University, thought that her son would be called immediately, before he could finish this academic year. She was quite hysterical about the prospect that a Japanese might be permitted to come here to more-or-less take his place. Numerous other people have spoken to me about the matter, and they all seem to feel about the same way.

... I am also sure that many people in Montana will be reluctant to send their children to college where Japanese students are invited or accepted. It is pretty generally felt that the American-educated Japanese have been largely responsible for the strategical advantage the Japs have had over us in this war.

Toole concluded his typewritten letter with the penned postscript, "In fact, there is just plain hell-to-pay in this town about Dr. Melby's statement." Subsequently Dr. Melby subordinated his principles to political realities: the university enrolled no Japanese-Americans for the fall term in 1942.

As barrister Toole noted, a related controversy had developed over the use of Japanese-Americans in Rocky Mountain agriculture. This situation began with the attack on Pearl Harbor and grew because of the ensuing anti-Japanese emotional fixation that gripped the West Coast. Although the FBI immediately arrested "enemy aliens" on its "suspect list," the federal government had developed no prewar plan to deal with the 110,000 *Issei* and *Nisei* in California, Oregon, and Washington.

As a result of concerted pressure from anti-Japanese organizations, however, the federal government adopted a policy of removal. On February 19, 1942, President Franklin D. Roosevelt signed Executive Order 9066. It authorized the evacuation of all persons of Japanese ancestry from "sensitive military districts" on the West Coast. Since approximately sixty-five percent of the Japanese-Americans affected were U.S. citizens, this fiat effectively stripped a significant ethnic group of its basic Constitutional rights. The President's action ultimately eradicated entire Japanese-American neighborhoods and farming communities.

Initially the federal government encouraged the voluntary migration of Japanese-Americans inland. Yet when pilot groups attempted to relocate inland, they met with intense racial hostility. So the majority of Japanese remained in coastal settlements, rather than lose their homes, businesses, and even their lives. As a result, on March 2, 1942, Lieutenant General John L. DeWitt, head of the Western Defense Command, issued the first of a series of public proclamations. It ordered the removal of "all persons of Japanese ancestry" from coastal military zones. The army hastily improvised fifteen "assembly centers"—i.e., temporary detention camps—within racetracks and fairgrounds to segregate the Japanese-Americans collected in its sweeps of coastal areas.

Then, on March 18, 1942, President Roosevelt issued Executive Order 9102. This edict authorized the construction of ten inland "relocation centers" to handle the more-than 100,000 Japanese-Americans incarcerated in the "assembly centers." The "relocation centers" were situated in remote areas of California, Arizona, Arkansas, Colorado, Idaho, Utah, and Wyoming. The government designed them as permanent internment camps, to hold Japanese-Americans for the duration of the war. So, by the end of May 1942, virtually all persons of Japanese ancestry had been removed from their homes on the West Coast and placed in the camps.

Early in 1942, Montana faced a national demand for greater production from mines, forests, and fields. Simultaneously, the war effort systematically was stripping the state of young men who performed many of these jobs. Montana's sugar beet industry, which had harvested 65,000 acres in 1941, proved no exception. Montana's beet farmers had committed to planting approximately 83,000 acres for the 1942 season, but thousands of young men were leaving the Hi-Line sugar beet districts, which stretched from Havre east to Culbertson. To compound the problem, the national draft rapidly was depleting the pool of transient beet-field workers whom Montana farmers usually employed during spring and fall.

Since the government held tens of thousands of Japanese-Americans in its inland "relocation centers," federal officials proposed the use of some of these detainees in the West's agricultural operations. The reaction of Montana Governor Sam C. Ford—who regularly exposed a fairly deep-seated anti-Japanese bias—to this idea was predictable: "From information received, the opinion here is *opposed* to the importation of enemy aliens [sic] into Montana to be used as agricultural workers."

The public opinion to which Governor Ford referred had been delineated in a February 28 editorial in the *Missoulian:*

> The West Coast is anxious to get rid of its Japanese. . . . At the same time, nobody else wants them, even in detention camps. Several hundred of them are confined at Fort Missoula now and appear to be a harmless lot, but Montana people do not like the idea of letting them work on the farms and in the woods of this district, on account of the fear of sabotage.
>
> . . . There is the prospect of a lack of labor in at least some of the western districts, and interned Japanese undoubtedly could be used to advantage—including their own advantage. But, unless the public mood should change, there is the definite prospect that this will not be done.

A Thompson Falls woman in a "letter to the editor" voiced an even more specifically anti-Japanese attitude held by many Montanans early in 1942. She was replying to another letter-writer's proposal that Japanese-American internees be imported to work on a forest road-construction project in western Montana:

> It is my opinion that the people of Montana should protest (and quickly) against any more Japs being sent in here, and then have the

ones who already are here put someplace where they can't do any damage. Our state has several industries that are vital to the national defense, and they will be blown sky-high.

Also, our forests and grain fields could easily be reduced to ashes, and our wild game could be eliminated completely, if those treacherous Japs came here and started their sabotage. For they are aware of how vital our industries are to the national defense. The people of Montana better wake up and realize the same thing—*and* do more toward preparing for our defense.

During the spring of 1942, however, such super-patriotic vilification of all Japanese began to wane in the beet-producing Milk River Valley. In Phillips County, for example, by early March, approximately a thousand men had departed to the armed services, and almost another thousand had left the area to work in war-production industries on the West Coast. At the same time, county beet producers had contracted to seed an acreage *twenty-five percent greater than the 1941 crop.* These farmers faced a critical labor shortage. Malta editor J. Russell Larcombe reflected the evolving change in their attitude:

Most of us are agreed these days that we should glance at our war situation with realism. . . . If that stand has any foundation at all, then why not extend it to the question of moving Japanese nationals and naturalized citizens into the Great Plains area from the potential combat zones and military bases of the Far West?

Newspapers of the area have, with one accord, jumped all over the proposal to send these people here. The words have been different, but the music has been the same—WE DON'T WANT 'EM!. . . . But why isn't it sensible to ship them to sparsely populated areas where they can be watched closely, where defense industries are few, and where army and navy drafts are making serious inroads on the labor supply? . . . As we see, it, it is possible to hate the innards of every Jap ever born and still make use of them.

The United States is widely reputed to be a practical nation and, as we view the matter, this is an excellent time to demonstrate it. Hate the Jap, if you will, but also admit that he is a good worker, a natural farmer, and a human commodity which this region is going to need if it is to continue as a substantial supplier to the war effort.

In response to Larcombe's suggestion, president of the Montana Federation of Labor James D. Graham and nine members of his executive board leveled charges: the sugar beet industry in Montana was not sufficiently important to the war effort to require such drastic action as the importation of Japanese-Americans; the use of Mexican labor as an alternative had not been investigated. To these statements, editor Larcombe replied most graphically:

We believe that the production of sugar is more important than Jimmy Graham understands. The sugar factories of this state—at Missoula, Chinook, Sidney, Hardin, and Billings—last year produced more than 2,500,000 100-pound bags of sugar. At the proposed rate of rationing, this means sugar for more than 10,000,000 persons each year. And we plan to increase that amount by 25 percent this season. Further, this sugar is all produced by what is conservatively estimated as 4,000 individual farmers in the state.

As to Graham's charge that alternate labor has not been investigated, we can only quote the sugar companies, who keep a close eye on the transient labor population. They say that the bulk of Mexican and Filipino workers who used to come to Montana are now either in the Army, or working at high wages in defense industries on the Coast, or replacing the Japanese evacuated from the farming areas of the West Coast. . . .

My own attitude is that, if Jimmy Graham or anyone else can show us another adequate source of field labor and *get it here by May,* when thinning should start, we'll eat something unpleasant and be glad of the chance!

And, before we gaze too fondly upon Mexicans from south of the Rio Grande, let us remember that, while the police blotters of Northern Montana won't show a single Japanese as having been jailed, for any cause whatever, in the last decade, they are all loaded to the guards with the names of our Mexican friends. Charged with what? Only with getting drunk on our streets, carving one another to bits with jackknives, raising marijuana behind their cabins, and teaching school girls the use of it! Ask any sheriff!

If necessity is the mother of invention, then it also proves a powerful modifier of group attitudes, even during wartime. The transformation of many Montanans' opinions that Japanese-Americans should be excluded from the state caused Governor Ford to retreat publicly from his earlier position—although he never personally abandoned his prejudices. In a news release from his Capitol office, the governor explained:

> Montana's farmers have reversed their earlier stand on the importation of Japanese farm labor from the Pacific Coast. They now are willing to take them. . . . I have received letters and petitions from virtually every section of the state asking that Japanese field hands be imported to help with the spring plantings and the fall harvests. . . . This change in attitude among farmers and others is the result of the realization that, unless sufficient labor is available, Montana cannot produce the extra sugar and other crops needed to help feed this country and its allies.

One of the most strongly worded petitions received by Governor Ford derived from a March 9, 1942, meeting of 175 farmers and townspeople in Malta. Representatives from throughout the Chinook sugar beet factory's district concurred that requesting Japanese-American workers from the "relocation centers" offered the most realistic solution to the labor shortage. When some beet growers declared that they lacked the housing for Japanese workers, Hatler Gearheart, the superintendent of the Utah and Idaho (U&I) Sugar Company's Chinook factory, promised that the company would provide low-interest loans for such housing construction.

Montana beet farmers recognized that most of the Japanese-American evacuees were U.S. citizens and retained the right to accept or reject the requested employment. Still, these cautious growers proposed some conditions for bringing the Japanese to the Montana fields: they would be paid only the standard field wage of $1.15 to $1.55 per harvested ton; they would be guarded closely at night; they would be kept from leasing or purchasing any Montana property. Although these proposals revealed a wellspring of anti-Japanese sentiment, they were superfluous: federal regulations required the payment of minimum wages for field work; guarding the Japanese-Americans field workers proved both unfeasible and unnecessary; Montana law prohibited the purchase of land by non-U.S. citizens.

In the Milk River Valley, however, timing became critical. Farmers had run well into the blocking-and-thinning season of May and June before even a token group of one dozen Japanese-Americans arrived from an "assembly center" near Puyallup, Washington, to assess the working conditions in Hill, Blaine, Phillips, and Valley Counties. So townspeople from Burnham to Tampico organized thinning brigades and closed their schools and businesses until noon each day, taking to the fields to help local beet growers.

In mid-June 1942, seventy-five Japanese-Americans from Washington arrived in Phillips County. They joined the townspeople, crews of Native Americans from several reservations, Work Projects Administration (WPA) workers, and schoolchildren in the fields. These evacuees noted that "more help would have volunteered from the detention camps, had it not been for rumors that workers accepting these jobs would be ill-treated in Montana." One week later, another group of sixty Japanese-Americans furloughed from the Washington center reached Chinook and located in beet fields down the valley.

As a result of assembling this patchwork labor force, farmers saved the 1942 sugar beet crop in the Chinook-factory district. Little additional beet work (except some hoeing) would be needed until the September-October harvest. The civilian volunteers returned to their jobs and homes, and some of the Japanese-Americans chose to spend the summer in their Washington camp. Joseph Beeson, of the War Relocation Authority (WRA) reported,

> About sixty-five Japanese workers in the Malta area—all but those who departed—have secured regular farm work here, on grain farms and in the wheat fields, and they won't be disturbed. The WRA is much pleased at the results of the experiment, as no difficulty was experienced with any of the workers. When harvest time comes, we expect that larger numbers of Japanese will come to the Valley, if they are wanted.

Suddenly farmers and ranchers all along the Hi-Line sought the Japanese-American workers. The Malta Commercial Club requested that a thousand-person Japanese "labor camp" be established in the abandoned Civilian Conservation Corps (CCC) buildings in the town's Trafton Park. Anti-Japanese war hysteria had been tempered by reality—although authorities never created that camp.

As the fall 1942 harvest began, the WRA's Joseph Beeson estimated that two thousand additional Japanese-Americans could be brought to the Montana fields, to join the three hundred who had spent the summer working in the state. At the same time, federal authorities signed an agreement with the Mexican government to import temporary farm labor from that country.

In the Milk River Valley, the need for additional field workers continued to grow, as the resident labor pool decreased due to enlistments, the draft, and high paying war-industry jobs on the West Coast. Early in September, fifteen Montana counties requested Japanese-American evacuee workers through the WRA.

During the autumn of 1942, farmers in Blaine, Phillips, and Valley Counties employed almost six hundred Japanese-Americans digging and topping sugar beets. Though this labor force was significant, it was not enough to harvest the estimated one million tons of mature beets. So authorities reactivated the makeshift springtime field army of volunteers.

From the state's stores, factories, offices, and schools, some 2,500 workers moved into the beet fields to dig and load the crop. Montana State College in Bozeman implemented a program that placed more than 800 college students in the Sidney, Billings, and Hardin beet districts. Although Montana's sugar beet harvest stretched into November, growers hauled better than ninety-five percent of the crop to the sugar-factory dumps before the ground froze.

The WRA praised beet growers in the Milk River Valley for their sensitive dealings with the Japanese-Americans during the 1942 season. Ed Berman, WRA regional director, observed,

> It is a most commendable handling of the situation, and these farmers' attitude will pay dividends to them in the years to come, when farm labor will be needed again. Many of the Japanese are willing to stay in the Valley during the winter, and anyone wishing to keep them as laborers may do so by obtaining permission from the Relocation Authority.

Nevertheless, by the end of November 1942, most of the Japanese-American field workers had returned to their "assembly" and "relocation" centers in California, Colorado, Utah, Idaho, Arkansas, Wyoming, and Washington. Among the exceptions were thirty-three workers whom the Great Northern Railway hired for the winter as section hands on its Montana mainline.

In summarizing the evacuees' impact on the Chinook factory's sugar beet crop, federal employment manager Wayne Fjosee stated,

> The Japanese worked for 59 different farmers during the season, thinning 808 acres and topping 1,309 acres of beets. Of the 2,117 acres of

harvested beets in the district, they worked on 1,907 acres. During the summer [between the beet-thinning and the topping seasons], some of the workers remained in the district and were employed in 538 different jobs, ranging from potato picking to grain harvesting to flock work. . . . The Japanese were most willing to work, and the district's farmers seem very well-satisfied with this form of labor.

The *Phillips County News* further observed,

Local people who made it a point to interview Japanese laborers this fall, regarding their impressions of this section, say that, almost without exception, the men spoke of the excellent treatment they had received from growers and citizens alike. And they said that they would be glad to work on next year's crop.

With this assurance of a somewhat stable labor pool, Hi-Line beet growers planned to maintain their 1942 production level for the 1943 season. These were brave, risky plans for farmers in a state that already had lost 40,000 residents to the armed services and about 25,000 to West Coast factories.

The impact of Japanese-American evacuees on Montana production never became as significant after the 1942 sugar beet season. Some *Nisei* remained in Montana during the winter of 1942-1943. Approximately 2,000 Japanese-American field workers joined them in May-June 1943 for the thinning season. In Phillips County, more than 150 evacuees returned—about 100 fewer than had worked the 1942 harvest in the county. Some of these Japanese-Americans continued to work on a straight wage basis, but others arranged sharecropping contracts with local beet growers.

The shortage in the 1943 beet labor pool was alleviated by the importation of Mexican nationals, by the relocation of some Italian prisoners-of-war, and by a group of white farm families who migrated en masse from Arkansas. However, neither the thinning nor the topping could have been completed without the field work of local civilian volunteers. The U&I Sugar Company also experimented with a mechanized beet topper and with several types of beet loaders in the Milk River Valley, in the hope of easing the labor shortage in the future. Further, in 1943, the company developed a system of sowing segmented seed, which decreased the amount of thinning necessary.

During 1943 Governor Ford continued his resistance to the placement of Japanese-American evacuees in Montana. Cloaking his personal prejudice in his usual guise of "reading public opinion," he stated,

> Undoubtedly opposition will continue in Montana to the purchase of lands by the Japanese—even though they are citizens of the United States. Reports to me indicate that opposition to the Japanese as residents of the state is decreasing. Still I believe that the solution to the farm labor shortage lies in importing Mexican nationals.

The rationale of state agricultural managers who favored Mexican labor showed some elements of the Governor's superpatriotic, anti-Japanese bias:

> Montana currently has about 700 Mexican nationals. Late in May, 1,237 of them were brought to Montana, under the arrangement between the U.S. and the Mexican governments. After the thinning work, however, several hundred were sent to Minnesota and Washington for field work.
>
> These workers are willing and easy to handle. *Most of them know no English and so they keep to themselves*—although some of the Mexicans are trying to learn enough English to get along.

At the end of the 1943 harvest season, about one-half of the four hundred Japanese-Americans in Blaine, Phillips, and Valley Counties returned to their "relocation centers." The balance—many of whom had sharecropped beets during that season—remained on the Hi-Line. These new residents, including some families, either leased cropland or purchased it from local beet growers. Slowly they began to be assimilated into Milk River Valley society. In the Chinook factory district, Montanans' experience with the Japanese-Americans had proved Governor Ford's public fears groundless.

During the 1944 and the 1945 sugar beet seasons, the role of the Japanese-American evacuees continued to diminish. In 1944 only 161 evacuees worked in all of Montana, and the figure dropped below 50 field laborers in 1945. Rather, authorities filled the necessary farm-labor pool with thousands of Mexican nationals, brought to Montana under a joint federal-state program.

When, in 1944, more than 4,000 Mexican laborers proved too few for the state's agricultural needs, the government transported about 2,500 Italian and German POWs to the Missoula, Billings, Hardin, Glasgow, and Chinook beet fields. For example, 250 German POWs disembarked from their special seven-car train at Chinook on October 20, 1944, and reportedly "goose stepped" to a hastily erected stockade within the county fairgrounds. That sight would not soon be forgotten by Blaine County residents.

In the Hi-Line sugar beet areas, Japanese-Americans became a part of the agricultural community, and they contributed just as other Montanans had to the Allied war effort. The extent of their assimilation is attested by a small item, hidden on an inside page of the Malta weekly paper on May 25, 1944: "The following Phillips County registrants have left for induction into the Army of the United States: Kiyoshi Tanouye, George Akira Sasaki, and Kay Kiichi Nakayama. The men are all American-born Japanese residing in Phillips County."

The story of the treatment of both the *Issei* and the *Nisei* in the United States during World War II includes sufficient shame for all Americans. Montana does not emerge as an exception to the national pattern. After the attack on Pearl Harbor, most Montanans developed a racist superpatriotism and a West Coast perspective on the war. Only very slowly did most Montanans learn to differentiate between Japanese-Americans and the Japanese military machine responsible for Pacific-theater warfare. Both time and reality were needed to mitigate their condemnation of *all Japanese.*

After more than a half century, we Montanans should be able to recognize the Japanese-American contributions to the state's war effort. As a people, we ought to confront our communal weaknesses as quickly as we praise our communal strengths.

CHAPTER 14

AVALANCHE ON
GOING-TO-THE-SUN ROAD

In the years since the 1933 dedication of Glacier National Park's Going-to-the-Sun Road, millions of motorists have thrilled in crossing the Continental Divide on one of the world's truly dramatic mountain highways. Indeed, they have experienced firsthand "the Alps of America."

What few of these holiday travelers realize, however, is the work that Park Service personnel expend each spring to clear the Trans-Mountain Highway of snow and debris. For months these men log double shifts, seven days a week, under dangerous conditions, to open the road for tourist traffic by mid-June. This job involves slicing through some snowdrifts as deep as seventy feet to reach the roadbed. Because of the park administration's continuous emphasis on safety, in only one of the more than sixty-five springs has tragedy struck these clearing crews. Yet, on that day in late May 1953, danger became disaster.

The official report of the incident, crafted by a National Park Service investigator, stated the case clinically.

On May 26, 1953, at about 11:30 a.m., there occurred on the Going-to-the-Sun Highway, at a point 0.7 of a mile above the Garden Wall Road Camp and almost 5 miles below Logan Pass, an avalanche which crossed the road and which killed two Park employees, injured one other very seriously, and buried yet another under approximately 7 feet of packed snow, from which he was rescued alive 7.5 hours later.

What this sanitized statement does not reveal are the circumstances that led to the tragedy, the ordeal of the men on the fog-shrouded mountainside, and the quiet heroism of several of the volunteer rescuers. That Jean Sullivan survived the avalanche—and soon returned to clear snow from the Going-to-the-Sun Road—serves as a testament to those National Park Service personnel who accept the challenge to punch their way through to Logan Pass each spring.

That breathtaking mountain pass sits at 6,646 feet, 1,150 feet above Upper St. Mary Lake to the east and about 3,500 feet above the westside Lake McDonald. Despite cool temperatures during the spring of 1953, snow-removal activities on the highway differed little from the ritual of the preceding twenty years. Plows had begun working along Lake McDonald in April and, by mid-May they had crossed Logan Creek and reached the westside loop. Beginning at that point, surveyors had marked the location of the roadbed beneath the snow mass. Bulldozers used the survey stakes to align their repeated cuts into the drifts until only a couple of feet of snow remained on the roadway. Operators then commenced the final clearing with huge, three-auger, rotary plows called "Snogos."

As the project progressed, however, the men encountered the heaviest snowpack in the roadway's history. Warming days and some light rains assisted the crews who worked on the heavy equipment in double shifts: from four in the morning until noon, and noon to eight o'clock at night. Still, they fell a bit behind the schedule that would open the highway by the unwritten deadline. Glacier Superintendent Jack W. Emmert noted, "Each year I have insisted that, during snow-removal operations, the men are to give safety first consideration. . . . But it is almost a case of tradition that all of the park is open to visitors by June 15."

AVALANCHE ON
GOING-TO-THE-SUN ROAD
May 26, 1953

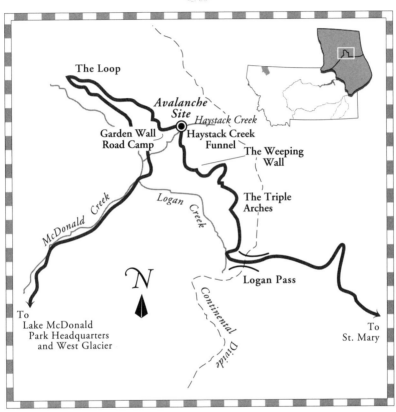

Unfortunately, weather conditions in mid-May conspired to delay clearing operations even more. A West Coast front moved in on May 21, bringing cloudy skies, light rain, and fresh, wet snow at higher elevations. Early on May 24, a two-day storm hit—dumping from four to twenty-one inches of that heavy, damp snow on the west side of the Continental Divide. As a result, Park Headquarters issued a press release:

> Snow-removal operations have been retarded because the crews repeatedly are required to retrace their operations and remove either fresh snow or snow that has covered the highway from small slide. Because of these unusual conditions, supervisory personnel have issued definite instructions that all the men in the snow-removal crews must not work in any location that appears to be exceptionally dangerous.

The terror of snowslides remained a constant companion of the crews, though each of the foremen on the 1953 detail held between fifteen and twenty years of experience in the springtime clearing of the Trans-Mountain Highway. So, when the storm began to clear on Tuesday morning, May 26, "mixed-gang foreman" Ray Price and his crew departed the Garden Wall Road Camp to survey the several slides that had covered the roadway between the camp and the Triple Arches.

In the damp morning fog, Price's men found that scores of small slides had swept down over the road, filling their earlier cuts with packed snow and debris. Because new, unstable, wet snow had fallen atop crusted snow surfaces above the road, the slides had happened quickly. They also had occurred in what the men recognized as normal slide areas—particularly in the Haystack Creek funnel, along the Weeping Wall, and just below the Triple Arches.

Between 8:30 and 10:30 on the rainy morning of May 26, Bill Whitford and Fred Klein attacked the remains of one new fifteen-foot-deep slide in the Haystack Creek funnel. Progress proved slow because the wet snow had packed heavily on the roadway. In fact, the slide was so tightly packed that, in two hours, the Snogo had cleared a cut through only about one-half of the 105-foot-wide slide.

At 10:30, road supervisor M. E. "Jean" Sullivan, age fifty-nine, and mixed-gang foreman George "Blackie" Beaton, forty-five, arrived at the slide in Sullivan's pickup truck from Park Headquarters in West Glacier, about thirty miles distant. Together Sullivan and Beaton could count nearly thirty-five years of experience clearing the Going-to-the-Sun Road. The two men sized up the situation. Since they had available no bulldozer to cut through the packed slide quickly, they decided to loosen the obstruction with dynamite so that the Snogo could handle the job easily.

When Whitford and Klein had worked the slide alone, Klein had served as Whitford's watchman, peering up the Haystack Creek funnel at the slopes above, in case another bank of snow broke loose in this slide-prone area. The slopes seemed stable as Whitford had ground the rotary plow again and again into his cut on the slide. With the decision to speed the job by blowing the packed snow, Sullivan unloaded fifty pounds of dynamite. He then sent Klein to collect the detonator caps from his pickup, parked on the road at the lower edge of the slide.

Meanwhile, Jean Sullivan assumed Klein's job of watchman—standing on the compacted snow near the recent Snogo cut. Foreman "Blackie" Beaton also took a watchman's position on the hood of the stationary Snogo truck. Bill Whitford sat in the driver's seat, prepared to move the Snogo if necessary.

Fred Klein never reached Sullivan's pickup. With no warning, a massive bank of snow broke loose above the roadway—not high in the funnel, where it could be detected early, but from a side slope beyond the men's view. In a matter of seconds, the avalanche slithered into the funnel and then rushed down the natural chute on top of the earlier slide. It slammed over the roadbed and on down the sixty-degree slope for several thousand feet. Sullivan recalled the details vividly:

I had asked Bill [Whitford], who had his head stuck out of the cab window, and George [Beaton] if they felt it was safe. George said, "Hell, yes, Jean. Let's blow it out and we'll be out of here in thirty minutes." He just got the words out of his mouth when I heard a little s-w-i-s-h. We call this kind of a quiet slide a "sneaker." I looked up and the snow slide was coming—no more than eighty feet above us—and I hollered.

The avalanche swept over the roadway, filling the Snogo cut and spreading wider than the original slide. It tossed men and machinery over the edge of the highway. In a wet mass of flying rocks, trees, bodies, and metal, the snowslide careened more than a half mile down the mountainside. That particular moment froze in Sullivan's memory.

To protect myself, I jumped into the hole that the Snogo had cut out, to keep myself from going down over the bank. When I jumped down, George [Beaton] was not over six or eight feet from me, and I saw him between the Snogo and the outside edge of the road.

When the slide hit the Snogo, I was not covered yet, and I heard the impact and saw the Snogo going over. It sounded like barrels of bottles being rattled. I know that Beaton was between it and the outside edge of the road, and Whitford was in the cab. There was snow in the air. Bill Whitford didn't have a chance.

After sending Freddie Klein after the [blasting] caps, I never saw him again on the job. I think that he was clear of the Snogo and almost off the old slide, on the way to my pickup.

As the rushing of the avalanche subsided and the air quieted, no sign of men or machinery remained on the highway—save Sullivan's pickup truck, parked just beyond the reach of the new slide's path. It seemed as if no one ever had been there, as if the slide found earlier that morning had not been touched—it just had grown wider and deeper and much longer. It was not yet noon.

Jean Sullivan recounted that timeless period of his entombment, before he lost consciousness.

> I was covered. I worked my head back and forth, and my hands a little. The snow was heavy. I thought of [my wife] May, but I wasn't cold or afraid for myself. I knew they would dig me out. I was worried about what happened to Whitford and Beaton, and I didn't know about Freddie [Klein]. It became hard to breathe. I kept breathing faster and faster and apparently I passed out.

*   *   *   *   *   *   *

Ray Price neither heard the avalanche nor saw the flying debris. He and Bill Dieringer had been working the other Snogo through a series of smaller slides on the roadway along the Weeping Wall, above the Haystack Creek funnel. At noon, foreman Price decided to walk the two miles down the road to see what had stopped the lower operation. He left Dieringer to rework one of that morning's cuts in a protected area. Price finally reached the Haystack Creek slide, but he could not decipher the confusing situation.

> As I climbed over the slide, everything looked just the same as when Bill [Dieringer] and I had walked over it that morning. Except that Jean [Sullivan's] pickup truck was sitting at the lower edge of the slide, with new snow up to it. I did not see the Snogo that Whitford and Klein were operating.
>
> I tried to figure out what had happened and why the pickup was there. It looked suspicious to me, as Jean wouldn't have left his truck if everything was alright.
>
> I decided that the other plow must have broken down, and that they took it back to the Garden Wall Road Camp to work on it. So I started walking down the road to the camp. Before I reached it, though, I met the afternoon crew hiking up from the camp to relieve the fore-

noon men. I asked them if they had seen my lower crew. They said that the rotary had not passed the camp that morning, and that, in fact, Jean Sullivan and George Beaton were on up above also.

Then I realized what had happened. Four men and a Snogo were buried on the road or were swept down the mountainside. From the camp I called the Chief Ranger's office and told them we needed all of the available men and equipment they could send—at once!

Price detailed one man to remain with the telephone at the camp. The foreman ordered him to maintain contact with headquarters and to alert the gravel crew working along the highway at Logan Creek to join the rescue operation. He then drove the four remaining workmen back up Going-to-the-Sun Road to the avalanche site in the Haystack Creek funnel. Rain fell lightly and banks of fog clung to the mountainside. It was 12:50 P.M.

Price posted a watchman near Sullivan's pickup. He then split the others into two-man squads and led them down off the road grade onto the steep, pock-marked avalanche face. Within minutes, one of the teams stumbled across a body only partially covered by the packed snow, near the edge of the slide, about five hundred feet below the road cut.

The four men frantically shoveled to uncover the body completely. Soon they could identify the watchman Fred Klein, and he was alive— but seriously injured and unconscious. After applying first aid and reviving him, the squads removed Klein to the side of the slide area. The four men then returned to the debris-laden avalanche face, encouraged that they might locate other survivors.

Within ten minutes, Price discovered Bill Whitford, the Snogo operator, about three hundred feet below Klein. Whitford had been thrown from the cab of the rotary as it tumbled down the mountainside, and he had been buried, except for the tip of his boot. The four shovelers worked rapidly but, when they lifted Whitford from the icy mass, it became obvious that he was dead. His chest had been crushed and his neck broken by the avalanche.

Although shaken, the men persevered: they still might find alive both Jean Sullivan and George Beaton. They must have been buried between the highway and the last battered piece of the Snogo, lodged in the slide about two thousand feet below the roadbed.

At 1:05 P.M., the first of the emergency forces from the valley arrived—the twelve-man gravel crew from Logan Creek. Within minutes, truckloads of park employees who had raced from headquarters reached the avalanche site. They carried shovels, probe bars, and first-aid equipment; they also brought front-end loaders to remove the probed snow.

In the meantime, Park Engineer Dick Montgomery organized the remaining rescuers systematically to probe and trench that part of the slide covering the highway in the Haystack Creek gulch. In the fog and drizzle, these men began at Sullivan's pickup and worked up the roadway, involuntarily casting furtive glances up the ominous funnel. Help continued to arrive between 1:30 and 3:00 P.M.—Great Northern Railway workers, private construction crews from a bridge project near Coram, equipment operators from Hungry Horse Dam, and private citizens from West Glacier, where Sullivan and Beaton were well-liked residents.

By midafternoon, more than fifty volunteers were searching for the two buried roadmen. At that point, Jean Sullivan had been covered by 7.5 feet of packed snow for more than four hours.

Park supervisors based their rescue plan on the assumption that the slide had buried Sullivan and Beaton in the shallower snow on the road's outer edge. Still, some of the rescuers disagreed with this approach to the trenching-and-probing scheme. One such dissident was Dimon Apgar, a lifelong resident of the area, a park service roadman, and a close friend of Jean Sullivan. The community of Apgar at the foot of Lake McDonald had been named for Dimon's father Harvey.

"Dimmie" Apgar played a hunch: he tried to recreate the avalanche in his mind, to place the four victims in the scene, and thus determine Sullivan's reaction. While running the scenario several times, Apgar noticed a slight overhang of snow along the inside edge of the highway, which the Snogo might have cut before the avalanche struck. In Dimon's mind, a man might have found some protection here from the impact of the snow.

So, for hours, while other rescuers probed the heavy, wet snow along the edge of the roadway, Apgar worked alone, digging exploratory holes and sinking his probe bar in the slide beneath this overhang.

After digging more than two dozen such holes, Apgar's hunch paid off—under more than seven feet of compacted snow, he uncovered the head of Jean Sullivan. And Sullivan was still alive! It was 7:00 P.M. before the rejoicing rescuers freed his entire body.

An ambulance whisked Sullivan down the highway to a Kalispell hospital. His discovery lifted the spirits of the volunteers, and they renewed their attempts to find George Beaton alive. With jerry-rigged lighting from Hungry Horse Dam, the men attacked the avalanche face into the drizzly night.

At 3:00 on Wednesday morning, May 27, Flathead County Sheriff Dick Walsh arrived at the avalanche site with George Talbott of Corvallis, Montana, and Talbott's bloodhound, "Joy." At first light, Talbott and Joy began systematically to crisscross the slide face below the roadbed. At 6:00 A.M., the bloodhound pinpointed a location about 1,200 feet below the highway, and a small crew of rescuers removed about three feet of snow that covered the body of foreman "Blackie" Beaton. The avalanche had broken his back and crushed the left side of his chest. A crew skidded this last body down the mountainside to the lower portion of the Going-to-the-Sun Road, where an ambulance waited.

By 9:00 A.M. all of the weary rescuers had withdrawn from the slide site. They had labored feverishly for more than twenty hours to save the lives of two of the avalanche's four victims. Dimon Apgar felt particularly rewarded.

Because of the abnormally heavy snowpack and continued rainy weather in 1953, park personnel did not open Going-to-the-Sun Road to visitor traffic until June 24. Supervisors assigned additional equipment to clear the road—attacking it from both sides of Logan Pass— yet the opening date proved the latest in the twenty-year history of the Trans-Mountain Highway.

Friends, fellow employees, and relatives held funeral services for Bill Whitford in Browning on May 29. Simultaneously, George Beaton's memorial services convened in Kalispell. The bloodhound Joy received a badge designating her "an official Park Ranger," in recognition of her work to locate the body of George Beaton.

Fred Klein never did recover fully from the injuries that he received from the avalanche. After extended hospitalization, he retired from the National Park Service on a full-disability pension. The most miraculous survivor, Jean Sullivan, spent three days in the Kalispell hospital then returned to assist in the clearing of the highway in June. After a full career, he retired. With his wife, May, Jean lived in the area until his death in 1972.

In the late 1960s—when May and Jean Sullivan would sit, side-by-side, holding hands before a crackling larch fire on an autumn evening—May could capture most succinctly the effect of the avalanche on Jean. "Before '53, there were times when Jean was just absolute hell to live with," she would say. "But after he'd been buried for seven hours on Going-to-the-Sun, he became a dear."

Particular events *can* alter one's perspective.

SOURCES AND SUGGESTED READINGS

Many of the following works served as sources for the chapters; some are primary sources, but all contain greater detail about the respective subjects.

CHAPTER ONE

SIR ST. GEORGE GORE: ELEGANT VICTORIAN AND SLOB HUNTER

Bradley, James H. "Sir George Gore's Expedition, 1854-1856," *Contributions to the Historical Society of Montana*, Vol. IX. Missoula: Missoulian Publishers, 1923.

Heldt, F. George. "Sir George Gore's Expedition," *Contributions to the Historical Society of Montana*, Vol. I. Helena: Rocky Mountain Publishing Company, 1876.

Ismert, Cornelius M. "James Bridger," in: LeRoy R. Hafen, ed., *The Mountain Men and the Fur Trade of the Far West*, Vol. 6, Glendale, Calif.: Arthur H. Clark, 1968.

Merritt, John I. *Baronets and Buffalo: The British Sportsman in the American West, 1833-1881*. Missoula: Mountain Press, 1985.

Roberts, Jack. *The Amazing Adventures of Lord Gore*. Silverton, Colo.: Sundance Publications, 1977.

CHAPTER TWO

THE THOMAS TRAGEDY ON THE YELLOWSTONE

Doyle, Susan Badger. "Intercultural Dynamics of the Bozeman Trail Era: Red, White, and Army Blue on the Northern Plains, 1963-1868." Ph.D. thesis, University of New Mexico, 1991.

Hebard, Grace R., and E. A. Brininstool. *The Bozeman Trail*. 2 vols. Cleveland: Arthur H. Clark, 1922.

(Helena) *Rocky Mountain Gazette*. August 11—October 6, 1866.

Small Collection 837: Samuel Homer Thomas Letter, Montana Historical Society Archives, Helena, Montana.

Small Collection 1303: Thomas Diary and Correspondence, Montana Historical Society Archives, Helena, Montana.

(Virginia City) *Montana Post*, May 10—September 27, 1866.

CHAPTER THREE

THE MASSACRE ON THE MARIAS

Bennett, Ben. *Death, Too, for The-Heavy-Runner.* Missoula: Mountain Press, 1981.

Ege, Robert J. *"Tell Baker to Strike Them Hard!"—Incident on the Marias, 23 January 1870.* Bellevue, Neb.: Old Army Press, 1970.

Ewers, John C. *The Blackfeet: Raiders of the Northern Plains.* Norman: University of Oklahoma Press, 1958/1985.

Gibson, Stan, and Jack Hayne. "Mayhem on the Marias," *Great Falls Tribune,* April 28, 1996.

Helena Weekly Herald, July 16, 1869—March 25, 1870.

Schultz, James Willard. *Blackfeet and Buffalo.* Norman: University of Oklahoma Press, 1962.

U.S. Congress:

    House Executive Document 185, 41st Congress, 2nd Session, *Serial Set #1418.*

    House Executive Document 197, 41st Congress, 2nd Session, *Serial Set #1418.*

    House Executive Document 269, 41st Congress, 2nd Session, *Serial Set #1426.*

    Senate Executive Document 49, 41st Congress, 2nd Session, *Serial Set #1406.*

Welch, James. *Fools Crow.* New York: Viking Penguin, 1986.

CHAPTER FOUR

LOST IN YELLOWSTONE: THE AGONY OF TRUMAN EVERTS

Everts, Truman C. "Thirty-seven Days of Peril," *Scribner's Monthly Magazine,* Vol. III, #1 (November, 1871). Also: "Thirty-seven Days of Peril," Montana Historical Society, *Contributions to the Historical Society of Montana,* Vol. V, Helena: Independent Publishing Company, 1904. Also: "Lost in the Wilderness, or Thirty-seven Day of Peril," *Montana: the Magazine of Western History,* Vol. VII, #4 (Autumn, 1957).

Haines, Aubrey L. "Lost in the Wilderness: Truman Everts' 37 Days of Terror," *Montana: the Magazine of Western History,* Vol. XXII, #3 (Summer, 1972).

Helena Daily Herald, August 15—November 15, 1870.

Langford, Nathaniel Pitt. *The Discovery of Yellowstone Park.* Lincoln: University of Nebraska Press, 1972.

Whittlesey, Lee H., ed. *Lost in Yellowstone: Truman Everts' "Thirty-Seven Days of Peril."* Salt Lake City: University of Utah Press, 1995.

CHAPTER FIVE

MONTANA'S WOLF WARS

Busch, Robert H. *The Wolf Almanac.* New York: Lyons and Burford, 1995.

Curnow, Edward E. "The History of the Eradication of the Wolf in Montana." M.A. thesis, University of Montana, 1969.

Hampton, Bruce. *The Great American Wolf.* New York: Henry Holt and Company, 1997.

Lopez, Barry H. *Of Wolves and Men.* New York: Charles Scribner's Sons, 1978.

McIntyre, Rick, ed. *War Against the Wolf: America's Campaign to Exterminate the Wolf.* Stillwater, Minn.: Voyageur Press, 1995.

CHAPTER SIX

LOUIS RIEL IN MONTANA: MÉTIS MESSIAH OR TRAITOR?

Flanagan, Thomas. *Louis "David" Riel: Prophet of the New World.* Toronto/ Buffalo: University of Toronto Press, 1979.

(Fort Benton) *Benton Weekly Record*, January 2—December 25, 1879.

(Fort Benton) *River Press*, October 27, 1880—December 21, 1885.

Helena Daily Herald, February 21, 1879—January 1, 1886.

Howard, Joseph Kinsey. *Strange Empire: A Narrative of the Northwest.* New York: William Morrow, 1952; and St. Paul: Minnesota Historical Society Press, 1994.

Huel, Raymond, ed. *The Collected Writings of Louis Riel.* 5 vols. Edmonton: University of Alberta Press, 1985.

Lussier, Antoine S., ed. *Louis Riel and the Metis.* Winnipeg: Manitoba Metis Federation Press, 1980.

CHAPTER SEVEN

HOGAN'S ARMY

Anaconda Standard, April 1—May 25, 1894.

Butte Bystander, April 15—May 19, 1894.

Butte Daily Miner, March 10—May 24, 1894.

Clinch, Thomas A. "Coxey's Army in Montana," *Montana: the Magazine of Western History*, Vol. XV, #4 (Autumn, 1965).

Helena Daily Independent, April 4—June 14, 1894.

Helena Daily Herald, April 21—June 15, 1894.

Northwest Industrial Army. *Keep Off the Grass*, Vol. I, #1 (June 1, 1894).

Schwantes, Carlos A. *Coxey's Army: An American Odyssey*. Lincoln: University of Nebraska Press, 1985.

CHAPTER EIGHT

THE REMARKABLE PETRIFIED MAN

Bogdan, Robert. *Freak Show: Presenting Human Oddities for Amusement and Profit*. Chicago: University of Chicago Press, 1988.

Bozeman Weekly Chronicle, September 7, 1899—January 24, 1900.

Livingston Enterprise, July 18, 1899—January 30, 1900.

New York World, December 31, 1899.

"The Wonderful Petrified Man," *Montana: the Magazine of Western History*, Vol. XII, #1 (Winter, 1962).

CHAPTER NINE

THE SWAN VALLEY TRAGEDY OF 1908

Anaconda Standard, December 31, 1908.

Finley, Mary Stousee. *The Story of the Shootings of Four Flathead Indians in the Swan River Area, Western Montana, 1908*. St. Ignatius: Louis J. Tellier, ca. 1960.

Helena Daily Herald, October 15, 1908—March 27, 1909.

Kalispell Bee, October 23, 1908—January 8, 1909.

Merriam, C. Hart. "Indians Killed by a Game Warden," *Forest and Stream*, Vol. 71, #12 (November, 1908).

(Missoula) *Missoulian*, October 15, 1908—March 25, 1909; April 9, 1972 [Mary Finley's account]; August 13, 1972 [Clarissa Paul's account].

Ronan Pioneer, October 15, 1908—January 8, 1909.

CHAPTER TEN

CARRY NATION VERSUS BUTTE, AMERICA

Asbury, Herbert. *Carry Nation: the Woman with the Hatchet*. New York: Knopf, 1929.

Butte Inter Mountain, January 20—February 16, 1910.

Butte Daily Miner, January 15—February 14, 1910.

Nation, Carry A. *The Use and Need of the Life of Carry A. Nation.* Topeka, Kan.: author, 1904.

Taylor, Robert Lewis. *Vessel of Wrath: the Life and Times of Carry Nation.* New York: New American Library, 1966.

CHAPTER ELEVEN

IMPEACHING JUDGE CRUM

Forsyth Democrat, August 10, 1916—December 27, 1917; January 2, 1919—December 30, 1920.

Forsyth Times-Journal, October 13, 1910—September 30, 1920.

Gutfeld, Arnon. *Montana's Agony: Years of War and Hysteria, 1917-1921.* Gainesville: University Presses of Florida, 1979.

Montana State Senate. *Proceedings of the Court for Impeachment, People of Montana against Charles L. Crum, March 20-22, 1918.* Helena: State Publishing Company, 1918.

Record Series 19: the Montana Council of Defense, Montana Historical Society Archives, Helena, Montana.

CHAPTER TWELVE

THE RONAN STATE BANK ROBBERY, 1929

Helena Daily Independent, June 15—November 20, 1929.

(Helena) *Montana Record-Herald*, June 18—November 21, 1929.

Hollingsworth, Vernon, "The Great Robbery," in: Velma R. Kvale, *Where the Buffalo Roamed.* St. Ignatius: Mission Valley News Printers, 1976.

(Polson) *Flathead Courier*, June 20—November 21, 1929.

Ronan Pioneer, June 13—November 21, 1929.

CHAPTER THIRTEEN

MONTANA'S WARTIME JAPANESE

Chinook Opinion, December 11, 1941—March 8, 1945.

Glynn, Gary. *Montana's Home Front during World War II.* Missoula: Pictorial Histories Publishing Company, 1994.

Havre Daily News, December 9, 1941—July 18, 1944.

(Malta) *Phillips County News*, December 11, 1941—March 22, 1945.

Manuscript Collection 35: the Governors' Papers, Box 107, Montana Historical Society Archives, Helena, Montana.

McCann, Kevin C. "Montana's Treatment of Japanese Americans during World War II," in: Robert R. Swartout, Jr., ed., *Montana's Vistas: Selected Historical Essays*. Washington, D.C.: University Press of America, 1981.

(Missoula) *Missoulian*, December 7, 1941—April 3, 1943.

Van Valkenburg, Carol. *An Alien Place: the Fort Missoula, Montana, Detention Camp, 1941-1944*. Missoula: Pictorial Histories Publishing Company, 1995.

CHAPTER FOURTEEN

THE AVALANCHE ON GOING-TO-THE-SUN ROAD

(Columbia Falls) *Hungry Horse News*, May 14—July 16, 1953.

Great Falls Tribune, May 20—June 7, 1953.

(Kalispell) *Daily Inter Lake*, May 25—June 3, 1953.

U.S. National Park Service, "Report on Avalanche Tragedy, 1953," File 801-01.2/X208-41, Ruhle Library, Glacier National Park, West Glacier, Montana.

ABOUT THE AUTHOR

Historian, researcher, writer, and teacher, Dave Walter has worked at the Montana Historical Society since 1979, and he currently serves as the Society's research historian. For the past fourteen years, he has contributed a regular history column to *Montana Magazine*, and his books include *Christmastime in Montana* (1990), *Today Then* (1992), and *Will Man Fly?* (1993). In 1994, the University of Montana conferred on him an honorary Doctor of Humane Letters. He lives in Helena with his wife, Marcella.

INDEX